St. Thomas Aquinas
Rescues Modern Psychology

Fr. Brian Mullady, O.P.

St. Thomas Aquinas
Rescues Modern Psychology

EWTN Publishing, Inc.
Irondale, Alabama

EWTN Publishing, Inc.

5817 Old Leeds Road, Irondale, AL 35210

Distributed by Sophia Institute Press, Box 5284, Manchester, NH 03108.

paperback ISBN 978-1-68278-283-5

ebook ISBN 978-1-68278-284-2

Library of Congress Control Number: 2022935767

First printing

Contents

St. Thomas Aquinas
Rescues Modern Psychology

Introduction

It is a distinct pleasure for me to write a book on the progress in interior healing that grace brings to the human spirit. This includes an introduction to the contributions of a man I never actually met but who has had an immense influence on my life, Dr. Conrad W. (Koert) Baars. He was born in the Netherlands on January 2, 1919, the second son, as he describes himself, of two affluent parents. Before the war he studied at Oxford and was taught philosophy by the famous Jesuit Martin D'Arcy. He lived through the horrors of World War II and spent several years in the concentration camp of Buchenwald, the price he paid for working for the French underground and helping Allied fliers escape. This experience was very influential in his future life. He survived his imprisonment almost miraculously and later immigrated to the United States. There he practiced psychiatry in various places, eventually ending up in Texas, where he died in 1981.

Dr. Baars counseled many priests and religious in his years as a psychiatrist. He and his colleague, Dr. Anna Terruwe, have the distinction of being the only psychiatrists to develop a theory of emotional illness based on Thomistic rational psychology. In these days in which people are often looking for guidance about psychological maturity as the foundational backdrop of the spiritual life, Dr. Baars' teachings seem a particularly timely contribution. Though some of them seem somewhat controversial, they are rooted in the best Catholic tradition. In his works, Vienna meets Athens and Jerusalem.

In the struggle to find the touchstone between faith and reason, modern psychology is often a very problematic area for Catholics. The reason is that post-Freudian psychology often sees the moral law embraced by Catholics as the seedbed that causes psychological illness. Dr. Baars was adamant that this is because modern psychology is based on a mistaken idea of the soul in which the spirit has no place with the passions or the emotions. The intellect and will become the enemy of psychological integration. Grace would destroy nature. One must be freed from morality to become whole. Dr. Baars clearly shows why this idea is mistaken and also why the best friend of emotional integration is the moral law and grace as authentically taught by the Church. For him, the best expression of this law is found in the teaching of St. Thomas Aquinas.

Besides his study of St. Thomas, the experience of Dr. Baars in Buchenwald was a major influence in his life and greatly affected his thought. He relates that one of the reasons he was spared is that he worked in the hospital. While there, he was secretly given the Blessed Sacrament by a priest and often distributed it to himself and to his patients. He relates in his autobiography, *Doctor of the Heart*: "Yes, I know I was totally unworthy to carry the Holy Host with me, even more so to touch it with my hands, but it was the only possible way of receiving Him whom I needed so badly in my misfortune. It was His continuous presence and His grace that carried me unharmed through the dangers of the long hours of my captivity. What this precious gift from Pere George had meant to me I cannot possibly describe. God does not leave His children when they are in need. And he knows only too well which of them, like me, need His help the most."[1]

His experiences in this concentration camp led him to appreciate his faith even more and to acquire a supernatural point of view about everything in life. This is crucial to understanding his work. He writes:

> One of the French priests imprisoned in the concentration camp of Buchenwald once said: 'When one speaks of the privilege to have come out alive from Buchenwald, one also should consider the fact that it has been a greater privilege to have been sent there, and even this, without the first, is a privilege indeed.'
>
> Yes, it has been a privilege, even though in the beginning I rebelled against God's holy will, and in my conceit demanded an answer as to why it had to be me and not my neighbor who had to undergo such misery. But, as time passed, my eyes were opened, and I began to see what before I could not comprehend. I had come to understand the real value of the things that I had once thought important and worth living for. When life was sweet and carefree, I had valued money, for example, because I thought it could buy me happiness; it could not, however, buy me freedom. The best of foods and wines and all the delicacies that please the tongue had also once seemed important, yet bread and water sufficed to keep body and soul together. I valued a carefree life, reaping the fruits of my education; however the miseries of prison life had taught me the real meaning of life. I had not valued God and his commands, but now

[1] Conrad Baars, *Doctor of the Heart*, New York: Alba House, (1996), 111.

in prison I realized that I could not live without Him—that life without God has no meaning.

Buchenwald was a hard and bitter experience, but it was an advantage to those who knew how to profit from it. Why does God permit wars and concentration camps? Again the answer is simple: because he loves us, because He wants to bring back to His fold those who otherwise in a life of pleasure and lusts would have been lost."[2]

These are certainly strange words for a psychiatrist, and they underline the reason why a study of Dr. Baars coupled with people like Aquinas and Teresa of Avila can be so beneficial to understanding the whole gamut of the relationship of religious experiences to the formation of the passions in the soul as well as the final perfection of human nature. Dr. Baars relates that he was practicing Freudian psychoanalysis for many years and was puzzled by the fact that so few people were cured by this method. Then he read a book which had a profound effect on his view of his science, *The Neurosis in the Light of Rational Psychology* by Anna Terruwe. In this book, Dr. Terruwe argued a position that Dr. Baars himself came to adopt in time. The clinical discoveries of Freud were brilliant, but his solution and explanation of the problem of emotional illness was very flawed because he was basing his therapy on a seriously flawed metaphysics of the human soul.

The findings of true modern psychology could only be adequately explained if they are based on an authentic picture of the human soul such as one finds in Aristotle and Thomas Aquinas. For example, the source of the classic neurosis cannot be found in a conflict of reason and the passions, but in an inadequate

---

[2] Baars, *Doctor*, 186.

penetration by reason of the passions because of a conflict within the passions themselves. Though bad moral education may be responsible for this unreasonable conflict, this conflict cannot be laid at the doors of morals itself, especially the authentic morals as taught by the Catholic Church. To deny oneself an emotional experience (sexual pleasure, for example) from a true choice based on the fact that the act used to procure it is a sin (against procreation or unity) does not create an emotional illness but rather the emotional maturity born from virtue. This maturity is essential for any authentic religious growth.

Drs. Terruwe and Baars were among the proponents of the idea that the West is emotionally bankrupt because it is spiritually bankrupt. This bankruptcy can be seen in practices like contraception, which they thought to be not only morally evil but emotionally destructive. Dr. Baars once said: "Birth control appeals so much to the selfish element in every human being. It eliminates the responsibilities and duties of love, it decries the consequence of romance, and it educates young people in their own selfish interest and in the indulgence of their selfish pleasures. France *[here he is speaking not of the French as people but of a movement to birth control in their country which was reflected in the disastrous murder of people in the concentration camp to eat]*, by destroying the morality of its youth, had led the way to the destruction of its own existence; it had removed in its children the backbone of perseverance against evil."[3]

My intention in writing this book is to offer the salient points of the teaching of Dr. Baars on the relationship of morals to psychology. As he guided many religious and priests in evaluating their vocation, it is hoped that his ideas will serve as at least a starting point for some serious questions involved in living and happy

[3] Baars, *Doctor*, 110.

Christian life especially for those in religious life and in religious formation. These teachings can also help the laity, both single and married, to more deeply understand what the demands of the formation of virtuous life are in responsible love. His funeral homily ended with words taken from one of his favorite authors, Gabrielle Bossis, in his 1948 book *He and I*, and can serve as an expression of what the love of divine grace offers us all in our vocations. In Bossis's book, Christ says: "And when I see you suffer, and suffer for me, I gather each of your sufferings with great love, as though yours were greater than Mine, and had a value that My heart would like to make infinite. And this is why, when you allow me to do so. I merge your life with Mine."[4]

This is, after all, what the spiritual life is about. As Teresa of Avila tells us, it is "a loving conversation among friends."

The reader will notice that the application of this study uses examples from the single vocation, marriage and the religious life. This is by design for several reasons. One should understand that because of the nature of the soul and the modern materialist culture the emotional and spiritual problems which result from this are a part of every vocation. One can see how authentic family life is the primary solution to the problem of man and how the wholesale approval and promotion in the contemporary culture beginning with the contraceptive pill has deeply affected the spiritual life of the contemporary world.

Also the reader will also note the lack of notes to the text. This is again by design since this book is a popular and not an academic book. It should be stated at the outset then that almost all the direct quotes not noted are to the works of Drs. Baars and Terruwe.

[4] Baars, *Doctor of the Heart*, viii.

The overarching theme of this book is that self-restraining love which is the cornerstone of both Aristotelean and Thomistic morals is the key to a recovery of all human healing of the spirit. Until schools and families return to teaching this, there will be no authentic or lasting peace of soul in the world. The warfare within sadly is always the source to the external warfare which plagues the human race. With weapons capable of destroying the planet, this dangerous world may finally bring about the greatest suffering yet experienced on earth. This is certainly not why God created the world. The teaching of this book are offered as one truly effective way not only to prevent this but is a proper foundation for the pursuit of truth and God in which alone man can discover his healing and his peace.

1

Normal Psychology

The "Tranquility of Order"

On the evening of that day, the first day of the week, the doors being shut where the disciples were for fear of the Jews, Jesus came and stood among them and said to them, "Peace be with you." When He had said this He showed them His hands and His side. Then the disciples were glad when they saw the Lord. Jesus said to them again, "Peace be with you. As the Father has sent Me, even so I send you." And when He said this, He breathed on them and said to them, "Receive the Holy Spirit; if you forgive the sins of any, they are forgiven; if you retain the sins of any, they are retained." (John 20:19-23)

What peace was the Lord speaking of here? Was it merely the peace that is the absence of conflict? If you go into a graveyard, there's no conflict. Everybody's at peace. Why? Because everybody's dead, there's no life. In the religious life, we often say that our most perfect community is the one that's in the cemetery, because everybody gets along in the cemetery! The Lord here was not speaking of a mere lack of conflict. He was speaking of a deeper idea. This deeper idea is reflected in the famous comment of Saint Augustine. This peace involves the *tranquilitas ordinis*, "the tranquility of order." And what order was the Lord speaking of here? The peace of the interior order, of a right conscience.

The tranquility of order of a right conscience is founded on truly being able to experience within us the order of our personality and all the powers of our soul. This is the wholeness of the unity of the passions, the intellect and the will, all powers that participate in any moral choice. This can only be brought to us by grace, by *sanctifying grace*. The Catholic doctrine concerning morality, which is reflected in the teachings of the popes and is based on Scripture, is the only way to truly express and fully experience this tranquility of order. But before we discuss this and its various ramifications, it's necessary to talk about what a human person has in their souls with regard to their various powers. Normal psychology of the natural picture of the soul must be understood before the abnormal.

Much of modern psychology tries to derive normal psychology from abnormal psychology, which is like trying to derive health from sickness and not the other way around. For Christians, the approach of modern psychology will not do because it is based on a faulty picture of the soul. It denies the spiritual part played by the intellect and will. Sickness must be understood in relation to health and not the other way around.

Dr. Conrad Baars pioneered a new approach to the study of psychiatry. He practiced Freudian psychology for years and discovered that very few people experienced a cure from psychoanalysis. He then read some studies by Dr. Anna Terruwe in which she maintained that the reason Freudian psychology was inadequate was because Freud's explanation of emotional illness was rooted in a wrong idea of the soul. There were two basic mistakes which were at the root of this erroneous explanation of the soul.

The first was that Freud tried to practice psychology by treating the soul as something material. The spiritual dimension of the soul rooted in the powers of the intellect and will was at least considered unimportant if indeed it existed. This had the practical result of making emotional health and healing hinge on removing the influence of the moral law from the interior life. Morals were viewed as an external imposition on the inner life and so as alien to the soul.

The second practical result was that abnormal psychology became the basis for developing normal psychology. In other words, how a man ought to be was decided in reaction to how he should *not* be. This, of course, is in direct opposition to people like Thomas Aquinas who maintain that in all science one must begin with being or nature and examine the lack of nature or sickness or evil in relation to what a thing is.

Dr. Baars read the aforementioned book by Dr. Terruwe and discovered: "Its content proved to be a pleasant surprise, for it confirmed a theory I had formed years before but which I had not been able to prove to my own satisfaction, namely, that many of the observations of clinical psychiatry may be best explained on the basis of Thomistic psychology, rather than that of other schools of psychology." The neo-Scholastic movement in the Church had been trying to show that also: "Scholastic psychology alone possesses at once a systematized body of doctrines and a framework sufficiently ample to embrace and synthesize the ever-increasing conclusions of the observational sciences."

Dr. Baars made it his mission in life to make the results of this happy collaboration available to those who participated in the social professions including psychiatrists as well as priests and those members of the clergy and religious life engaged in spiritual direction and formation. He implemented the statement of his collaborator in this: "Rational psychology had been for me the key to an entirely new insight into the nature of the neurosis and, at the same time, to an entirely justified and successful method of therapy."

There are some people who have tried to integrate Dr. Baars' ideas with their practice of counseling and at times have found great difficulty in doing this because his ideas presume a knowledge of both modern psychiatry and Aristotelian philosophy. The former is more easily acquired than the latter today. Since normal psychology should be the basis and standard of judgment for abnormal psychology, a quick overview of Thomas Aquinas' theory of the soul would seem in order.

Thomas Aquinas followed Aristotle in his teaching on the soul. For Aristotle, the soul was one principle that was in a substantial union with the body. The two were not principles in merely an incidental or even antagonistic union as Plato taught. They were equally important component aspects of the same reality: human nature. The Church has accepted this way of looking at things. "The union of the soul and body is so profound that one has to consider the soul to be the 'form' of the body, i.e., it is because of its spiritual soul that the body made up of matter becomes a living, human body; spirit and matter, in man, are not two natures united, but rather their union forms a single nature." (*Catechism of the Catholic Church*, n. 365)

The human soul forms the one basis for all the movements that characterize human nature. Traditionally these are considered to be three: the kind of movement man shares with the plants shown in reproduction, growth and nutrition (vegetative life); the kind of movement man shares with the animals in both knowledge that comes from the senses and sense desire shown in the passions (sensitive life); and the kind of movement which is unique to man shown in the presence of the intellect and will (intellectual life). The vegetative life has nothing to do with spiritual growth because there are no powers of knowledge and desire on this level of existence. Yet things that happen in the intellectual and sensitive life can affect our vegetative powers (e.g., sadness can slow down metabolism, anger can speed it up or make the face flush). Things like blood pressure or blood sugar can affect the emotional or intellectual life, but there is no power of knowledge or desire in these, and so in themselves they are not a part of the issue. The unity of the soul is what causes this experience.

The unity of the soul is also at the basis of the mutual influence between the moral life and the life of the passions. Modern psychiatry would deny this influence. Dr. Baars believes it is intense. In fact, it is errors in the intellect, mistaken ideas of the truth about man, that not only cause an evil moral life but also impair healthy maturity in the emotional life. For Baars, contraception is not only a sin, but it also causes emotional illness.

Normal psychology, which is at the basis of the development of man, presumes a true understanding of human nature. Dr. Baars is clear that in at least one of the principle experiences of emotional difficulties — repressive neurosis, where a patient seeks to remove harmful emotional experiences from consciousness — therapy must be based on trust. There are two causes of lack of trust, one of which is emotional and the other of which is intellectual.

Two kinds of causes may be responsible for fears in neuroses due to repression: either a mistaken understanding of moral obligation, or certain concrete facts that initially aroused these fears. To the first category belong false notions of morality (the nature of God, the relationship between man and God, sexuality, religious duties, etc.).

The second category comprises such concrete factors as fear-producing conditions in which the patient is brought up (a father who was too strict or a cruel, fault-finding stepmother), or certain childhood experiences which, combined with generally mistaken notions, stimulated fear unduly.

Dr. Baars places the nature of emotional illness not in the conflict between the intellect, will, and passions, as often occurs with modern psychology, but in a conflict *within the passions themselves* that cannot be resolved because it is based on one of the two factors mentioned above. The true issue, then, in approaching mental health is first to identify how such a conflict can occur within the passions themselves and why willpower cannot resolve such a conflict.

Many well-meaning educators and religious formatters who deal with those who practice clearly abnormal behavior think that if they can just educate the person and stimulate a person's will, that that person can overcome the strange behavior. This is simply not the case, because though the conflict is often caused by bad morals education, the issue must be resolved in the passions—something the patient simply cannot do by willpower alone.

The point of psychological therapy is not to free a person from morality in order to reduce the emotional pressure of impossible demands from without, but rather to free a person for morality by untangling the interior web spun from years of bad teaching or practice. Concomitantly, good formation of the passions through education and freedom, along with good encouragement to the right kind of self-restraining love based on the person's age and temperament, is the best defense against the development of emotional difficulties. This is very far from good training, which could be merely stimulus and response, and truly involves stimulating the intelligence and desire of the subject so that he or she can make good choices.

Later, it will become evident how important this intellectual and moral development in a normal, gradual, and loving way is for living Christian surrender and detachment. The intellectual and moral formation must be gradual. If it is either expected too early or demanded too late, then it is difficult for the person being formed to develop normally. Moral actions will not flow from a unity of intellect, will, and passions, but rather will be more the result of desire to relieve passions that are either malformed or out of control. Though Catholics know that nature is wounded by sin, nature is not totally depraved and still has a basic orientation toward good. This realization must be begun in early childhood development. Man, by nature, is wounded but fundamentally oriented to the goodness and love of God.

The essence of a healthy upbringing is an attitude on the part of educators that is in fundamental agreement with that of God. This means that they respect the child's need to become a free human being and abstain from anything that will interfere with that freedom, such as the undue stimulation of potentially repressing emotions or sin in morals. This they can do only if they have a reasonable trust in the basic goodness of every human being, i.e., that man has continued to be oriented toward the good in spite of the imperfection of his nature caused by Original Sin.

Man as Body and Soul

Man is normally considered—in religion, at least, and in authentic philosophy, I maintain—to have a spiritual dimension and a physical dimension. The physical dimension we can see in the body; the spiritual dimension we can perceive according to man's actions. The question has always been, "How do these two dimensions relate to each other? Are they in opposition to each other? Is one more necessary than the other? Just what is the relationship between the two? And in their relationship with each other, how can we experience what the various powers of the human soul really are that all have to be fulfilled by some kind of activity?" This, in turn, will lead us to discover what kind of actions could fulfill us and, therefore, what experience is necessary for us to have the tranquility of order inside.

Another word for the tranquility of order would be "integrity." In what does the final integrity of man consist?

In the history of thought—in Western philosophy at least—there have been two basic tendencies or errors with regard to this problem of the relationship of the body to the soul. One is to reduce man to his material or physical dimension. The other is to reduce him to his spiritual dimension.

Material Man

The first of these two tendencies was reflected in the ancient world by materialists like the Greek philosopher Democritus, who in the fifth century B.C. tried to reduce man to a collection of atoms. In other words, the body is all there is to man, because there is no spirit or soul. We are only material beings. This position, of course, is very difficult to maintain, because we can actually examine in us a whole dimension of life that's different from merely being a body.

It's true that we have certain characteristics that are like physical bodies. After all, if we jump off a cliff, we fall like a stone. But there's also a dimension in us that isn't explainable merely by the collection of atoms within us. This dimension borders, first of all, on the emotional—a trait we share with the animals—but it also borders on the spirit. There is a dimension in us, a way of knowing, which is very different from the animals' way of knowing. We call this the *intellect*.

Plato, a Greek of the fourth century B.C. who was the first great philosopher to discover the spiritual soul, then began to have difficulties with the body. He reasoned that if man is a spirit—if there's something immortal about us—then how do we explain our relationship with the body? Plato thought that we existed before our birth in this ideal spiritual world with no bodies and then sort of fell into matter when we were born. For Plato, matter was like a prison that held us bound, and the only way that we could truly be ourselves was to escape from matter. In order to do this—in order to understand or to know or to love—it was necessary for us to completely deny the material dimension to ourselves.

Some aspects of Christianity have this as a basis—when people suggest, for example, that feelings or emotions have absolutely no place in a virtuous person, that they need to be stoically destroyed and denied as though they didn't exist. In my opinion and in the classic Catholic position that I think does justice to the human person and to Scripture, neither one of these positions really serves, because we notice that our body and our spirit have a necessary relationship to our integrity. More than that, all the various dimensions that are within us are not simply separate experiences that have no relationship to each other.

Plato—again because of the way he thought about knowledge and things—believed that if men indeed had souls, that there were three parts or dimensions to our souls. One part corresponds to the life we shared with the plants, the appetitive part: when we eat, we grow (sometimes too much), and when we drink, our thirst is slated, and the water becomes a part of our cellular life or organic life. Another part to our soul we share with the animals is the emotional, which is the ability to feel, to have emotional experiences, to experience love and hate. The third part, rationality, is ours uniquely: in Christian terms, we might say that we share it with the angels.

An Absolutely Necessary Relationship

So, for Plato, we were like a microcosm of the whole world comprising three parts to our souls. The body was like a ship, and these parts of the soul were like the sailors, each contributing to the sailing of the ship but with no necessary relationship to each other. However, that is not our experience. If I have a headache, it's difficult for me to think. If I am crying, it's difficult for me to focus sometimes. If I am thinking deeply about something, I might not be aware of pain. In other words, there's a real relationship between how our bodies are constituted and these "parts" to our souls. They overlap. As a result, they can't be like separate dimensions, like three stones in a pile that have no necessary relationship to each other, or like sailors in a ship that have only a moral unity of acting by steering the body instead of a real unity with the body and among one another. Put succinctly, the soul and body have a union in acting because they have a union in being.

The body and the soul are in *absolutely necessary relationship* to each other. And as a result, man is neither "just matter" nor "just spirit." He is a composite of both. As a result, to experience integrity, justice must be done to all of these various aspects of the human person.

Plato and Democritus exemplified these ways of thinking of the ancient world, but there is a similar way of thinking in the modern world. Those of us who love Thomas Aquinas and date the modern world from the sixteenth century realize that by the eighteenth century there was again a whole way of thinking in Europe that tended to reduce us to mere matter. We have this in modern science today: the human person is looked upon merely as a collection of atoms and molecules, and our psychology or our interior life is reducible, for example, to what will make us emotionally happy. This reflects Democritus's way of looking at things in the contemporary world, and it is insufficient. It is insufficient for morals, and it fails to explain the fullness of the human person. Ancient atomists such as Democritus as well as many modern thinkers and scientists who want to reduce our knowledge to merely physical description have likewise tended to reduce man or the human person to mere matter.

Spiritual, But Not Material

The second tendency, which is just the opposite of that of materialist thinkers, is to try to reduce us in our integrity to only spirit. Plato is an example of this in the ancient world. But in the contemporary world there are also examples of thinkers who have tended to suggest that the material side of man has nothing to do with his understanding of the truth. In other words, our experience of the tree outside of us has nothing to do with our ability to explain what a tree is, or our experience of ourselves by what we can observe with our five senses has nothing to do with explaining what a man is. Instead, we find it all within.

In this way of thinking, we become our own life project whereby we create ourselves by our choices and our options. There is no objective human nature; the source of human nature is not something one can examine and discuss with other people. It depends on how we feel about it. We've all heard someone say, "If it feels right, do it. How can it be so wrong if it feels so right?" Everything is created by our own subjective needs.

This tendency also is an error. Obviously, it doesn't do justice to the fact that we do notice certain common characteristics about our humanity. It's not possible for us to sacrifice the spirit to the body, or the body to the spirit. Nor is it possible for us to say, with Plato, that we have these various powers within us that have no necessary relationship to one another. For example, in this way of thinking, in order for us to become integral we have to deny our passions so much as to completely destroy their existence.

C.S. Lewis, the famous English author, wrote *The Screwtape Letters*, a fanciful correspondence from a senior tempter in hell to a junior tempter on earth about how to tempt someone away from Christianity. Lewis had the devil say, "Never forget that when we are dealing with any pleasure in its healthy and normal and satisfying form, we are, in a sense, on the Enemy's ground. I know we have won many a soul through pleasure. All the same, it is His invention, not ours. He made the pleasures: all our research so far has not enabled us to produce one."[5] God made the pleasures; God made the passions. He made food taste good because if it didn't taste good, we'd die. We wouldn't eat.

You can see here the necessary relationship between the body and the soul. God made the sexual act feel good. Why? Because if not, nobody would ever have any babies, nobody would ever get married; He wouldn't be able to people heaven with those that were made in His image and likeness. So, it's necessary for us to say that if there are all these powers of the soul, as Plato maintained, that they must be in necessary connection with one another.

The "Powers" of the Soul

The way that this has normally been put in Christian history using philosophical terms—you can find this in the *Catechism of Catholic Church* (no. 365)—is that the soul in man, which is spiritual, is related to the body in man, which is material, as a form is to matter; in other words, the soul is the form of the body, not the other way around. What implication does this have for what these powers of the soul are?

---

[5] Lewis, *The Screwtape Letters*, Letter IX.

Generally speaking, we can say that there are four basic kinds of powers in men, three in the soul and one that is just material in the body. Our bodies share characteristics with every other body, as in our earlier example of dropping a body off a cliff. We also share organic life with the plants. We also share the ability to know in a sensible way, using the five senses. We also feel like the animals do: we feel love, hate, anger, joy, and sorrow. In addition, we notice that we have other powers distinct from the animals. We have the ability for self-determination, and we also have the ability for self-knowledge, for reason. You can train a dog to fetch a sponge in order to wash your car, but if the sponge isn't there, the dog can't reason, "Well, a cloth is just as good as a sponge, and therefore, I'll fetch a cloth." The dog has no ability to reason, and he does not have a kind of knowledge that goes beyond the order of the senses to experience intelligence and reasoning. Man *does* have the ability to reason because in addition to sense knowledge he has a spiritual soul and a spiritual kind of knowledge.

Therefore, we can say that there are three basic powers to the human soul, which must be enumerated again. They are nutritive powers in the body, the sense powers, and the spiritual powers. There's the power he shares with the plants: growth, nutrition, reproduction. There's the power he shares with the animals: to experience sense knowledge and sense joy, satisfaction with food, good taste, and so on. Finally, there's the power man experiences in his spirit, which we'd characterize as in relationship to the angels as pure spirits, as we'd say in Christianity and Judaism.

These powers, then, are all necessary to explain what a human person is.

Human Integrity and Peace

The Book of Genesis tells us that man is created in the image and likeness of God. What that means is that each individual human is created with a body and a spirit in the image and likeness of God. Our spiritual soul is influenced by, and has an influence on, the life we share with the plants, the life we share with the animals, and the life we share with the angels and with God. It's absolutely necessary for us, then, to say that human integrity involves having a complete integration of all these powers together—a unity. This integrity especially demands that those powers that relate to our moral selves must not be in conflict with one another but rather must be at peace with one another.

It is this peace that the Lord was speaking of in the Upper Room, when twice He said, "Peace be with you" (John 20:19ff). He showed the Apostles His hands and His side. Here we have the body again relating to the spirit. The body is not evil, it is good: God has created it. It is this peace the Lord was speaking of when He breathed on the Apostles and gave them the Holy Spirit. It is this peace that is finally experienced in the resurrection of the dead, when our bodies and souls will be reunited for eternity.

We have to consider this so that when we notice these powers are in disarray, we know we need to experience the true healing of our spirits. After all, most of us have to admit—and if we don't admit it, we're in denial—that there is warfare going on within us, a warfare between what we feel and what we know to be true. Saint Paul reflected this when he said, "For I do not do the good I want, but the evil I do not want is what I do. Wretched man that I am! Who will deliver me from this body of death?" (see Rom. 7:19, 24). And then he says, "But thanks be to God and Our Lord Jesus Christ" (see Rom. 7:25). The healing of the spirit, the healing that began in its fullness when the Lord breathed the Holy Spirit on the Apostles, is the source of that true relationship of all of these powers in the soul to each other so man can experience the integrity internally which was lost in the Original Sin.

Man on the Horizon

What is the one experience that can bring peace to our hearts and to our character? What is the only experience that does justice to the body, to the vegetative life, to the sensual life, and to the life of intelligence, and tries to show how all three of those things in the soul can truly act in harmony with each other? It is the Beatific Vision. Sanctifying grace is necessary to arrive at it.

In the next chapter, we will discuss how grace relates to all these powers but especially to the powers we share with the animals, the sensitive or emotional power, and the powers we share with the angels, the intellectual or rational power, because this is the place where the actual warfare occurs. After all, our bodies don't really desire anything in themselves; instead, we have to look to these powers to identify our desires.

An ancient saying expresses the basis for human integrity and peace of soul: "Man stands in the middle of creation between flesh and spirit, between time and eternity." Man is on the horizon of being. If you look at a horizon, you see air above it and land below it. We stand on this horizon. We have a foot in both matter and spirit. To experience true human integrity, it is necessary for the Holy Spirit to enter the entire person through the intellect, will, and passions.

2

Original Integrity

"Until They Rest In Thee"

Thus far we have discussed the various goods involved in the perfection of the human spirit. We have seen how even pagan philosophers understood that because of the presence of intelligence in us, it is simply impossible for us to experience integrity, the quieting of our spirits, without our communion with God. As Saint Augustine says, "Our hearts are restless until they rest in Thee."

We can enter a certain communion with God on this earth through grace, but a perfect communion with God cannot be completed until we see God in heaven, when we will know Him directly even as we are known, "face to face" (1 Cor 13:12). Saint Augustine has a famous saying in his *City of God*: "There we shall rest and see, see and love, love and praise. This is what shall be in the end without end." Our desire for good will come to "rest and see," because we will experience the Good—"Good" with a capital "G." We shall "see and love," because all of our loves will be finally stilled in the one love, which alone is necessary. We will "love and praise," for "this is what shall be in the end or purpose without end." There is the final perfect act of the intellect. So, this experience is the necessary basis for the final integrity of the soul—or its completion, its peace, its healing—that we should experience here on earth. It was to obtain this perfect act that God created us in the state of grace.

Human intelligence has this enticement to know the "why" of the world, a trait evident in the questions raised by little children. I have known newly ordained older seminarians who have said: "I've been a pastor for a whole year, and no one has ever asked me a theological question." One of the priests present who heard this leaned over to me and said, "Evidently, in the year he's been a priest or pastor, he's never talked to any of the children in his parish, because they ask nothing but theological questions. 'Why does the sun rise?' 'Why does the rain fall?'"

It is this fact that led Aristotle to begin his *Metaphysics* with the statement: "All men by nature desire to know." This desire to know is rooted at the depth of the human spirit. He then goes on to say that this leads to wonder at the causes of the world, and that wonder gave rise to philosophy as a study. Wonder at nature is what first caused people to begin to think deeply, and that deep thought cannot be stilled until we know the ultimate explanation.

In Christianity, of course, we know the ultimate explanation is nothing less than God. Doesn't Jesus say, "And this is eternal life, that they know thee the only true God, and Jesus Christ whom thou hast sent" (John 17:3)? In this knowledge, our love is stilled, our desire to go out of ourselves for the good. This desire, this fulfillment in knowing God, demands grace. We obviously cannot arrive at knowing an infinite being without help from that same Infinite Being—and this is true regardless of the existence of sin. Grace is necessary for the perfection of nature. Grace is the fulfillment of normal psychology.

A Communion of Persons

Before the introduction of sin, man has needed grace to go to heaven. This was true of Adam and Eve before the Original Sin. What were the characteristics of Adam and Eve's life? We'd know that Adam and Eve were created in the state of grace. Why do we know this? Remember that Adam had the animals brought to him to be named, and he gave each one its name. "The man gave names to all cattle, and to the birds of the air, and to every beast of the field; but for the man there was not found a helper fit for him" (Gen. 2:20). Why not? Because there was no other being that was of spirit and flesh to whom he could give himself. "So the Lord God caused a deep sleep to fall upon the man, and while he slept took one of his ribs and closed up its place with flesh; and the rib which the Lord God had taken from the man he made into a woman and brought her to the man" (Gen. 2:21-22). Adam experiences a kind of second creation. In this second creation, a part of his flesh—his rib, to show that this person is an equal to him—is taken out of him and made into woman. Then Adam is given this second person with whom he will be able to have a relationship, a communion of persons. If man is made in the image and likeness of God, then he must be able to experience a communion with other persons as the Trinity does.

Adam sees Eve. He names her as he did the animals, but he cries for joy because he is no longer alone. She accepts being named as one like him, and they experience this relationship of a communion of persons to each other. Adam has an infused knowledge, a special knowledge, a special grace given to him. He did not have to do any scientific experiments to discover the fact that woman is different from all the other creatures he has named. He has an experience and a knowledge given to him by God. He also experiences a loving obedience. He experiences the fact that he was called to a kind of self-determination: God had told him, "You may freely eat of every tree of the garden; but of the tree of the knowledge of good and evil you shall not eat" (Gen. 2:16-17). Adam has a free and loving relationship with Eve that is all gift and reception. They both first have communion with God by sanctifying grace and then with each other. They are "both naked, and were not ashamed" (Gen. 2:25).

Integrity of the Passions — And its Loss

After they committed the Original Sin, however, Adam and Eve become ashamed of their nakedness. They questioned the freedom and love of the gift and so the benevolent love of the giver. Since the gift of grace depended on their obedient love, they lose grace. Selfish egotism enters their relationship. What has changed between their condition before the sin and their condition after the sin? The flesh had not changed, but their relationship had changed. Before the sin, they had no fear of extortion in giving the gift of themselves. They not only had a loving obedience, but they actually enjoyed it—their passions were one. Their passions were focused. Their passions were integral. Their passions could not lead them to want to manipulate, use, or abuse another human being. In other words, they experienced integrity with regard to their passions. They could be standing in each other's presence naked because the human body is good, not evil. It expresses the nobility of man.

Consider Michelangelo's *David* and compare it to a pornographic representation of the human body. The difference is that one seeks to express the nobility of the spirit while the other seeks to call forth manipulative, lustful, sinful desires. Adam and Eve had an easy virtue because their emotions were one with their intelligence and their wills. Grace caused this. In their bodies, they had the ability to die, but God exteriorly protected them so that this ability to die would not be something that they'd experience—especially the corruption of death, which is something we all fear.

What implication does this have for the integrity of man? Loving obedience is not ordinary obedience. We could be obedient and still look at obedience as an external imposition on us because we don't understand the reasons why we're supposed to do as we are instructed. In loving obedience, we not only do what we're told, but we also interiorly experience this obedience because we actually love the good that is offered to us. In other words, our wills become identified with the will of the person who asked us to do the thing because we experience the common truth through our intelligence.

Man is elevated to experience intimacy with God, and therefore is made a son or daughter and heir. However, man became a slave through Original Sin because he didn't experience intimacy with God anymore. He lost grace. Adam and Eve were created in grace, which gave them the ability to look at the world from God's point of view. This gave them the ability to experience time from eternity. They also could look at each other from God's point of view, and this was expressed in their sexuality. They truly demonstrated what the sexual urge is made for in man. The sexual urge arises in us at puberty, at a time when, for the first time, our emotions are all drawn toward another. Emotions which are expressed as "me" and "mine" are more characteristic of children; yet when sexual desire arises in us at puberty, we desire the good of "him" or "her." It's generally the first place where a child's world moves beyond itself as a good and truly experiences the good of another human being as its own.

In other words, the sexual urge is not something that is primarily physical or even emotional, but rather something moral and personal. This urge is an immature but real desire to look on another's good as one's own. Adam and Eve experienced this without the possibility of manipulation because they were in the state of grace and there was no sin. It wasn't possible for them to use or abuse another human being for selfish purposes because each of them was filled with God, and they expressed that fulfill-ment and fullness of God through grace in their relationship with each other. They truly regarded the world and each other from a supernatural point of view.

Original Justice, Original Integrity

This condition of Adam and Eve is often called *original justice* because they were right within. It's also called *original integrity* because their bodies perfectly served their passions, and their passions perfectly served their intellects and wills. Their intellects and wills perfectly served God. Adam and Eve, therefore, are commonly said in Catholic theology to have enjoyed three gifts in their original creation. These gifts reflect true human integ-rity because they reflect all the various powers of the soul—the body, the passions, the intellect, and the will—and their proper relationship to God, which is the only final good that can sustain and fulfill them.

The first are the natural gifts—the intellect, the will, the pas-sions, and the body. The intellect is naturally drawn to truth; the will is naturally drawn to good. The passions are naturally drawn to two individual goods, just as they are in animals. Because of the presence of the Spirit in us, they are also naturally born to be obedient to reason because that's the higher faculty of man. As a result, passions that are unruly are inhuman passions. Pas-sions that are ruled by reason are human passions. This is a very important distinction.

The body experiences this communion. In the beginning, before sin, the body experienced a tendency toward serving these gifts and thereby was preserved from death. This preservation was based on grace and on obedience in love to God, who externally protected the body. Once grace is lost though disobedience, the body no longer experiences divine protection and communion of life through the soul. This lack of integrity in the soul leaves the body to its natural tendency—like all matter, to death.

Sanctifying Grace

In addition to natural gifts, Adam and Eve also experienced the supernatural gift of grace, *sanctifying grace*, in their state of original holiness. In Catholic thinking, sanctifying grace is a true change in the very nature of our soul—which, in the words of the Second Letter of Peter, allows us to become "partakers of divine nature" (2 Pet. 1:4). In other words, when Jesus said, "Receive the Holy Spirit" (John 20:22) and breathed on the Apostles in the Upper Room, they experienced a gift that was added to the very nature of their souls. In philosophical terms, we call it "the essence of their souls" that is elevated so that they could experience communion with the Trinity. In the case of Adam and Eve before sin, this reception of the Holy Trinity in the soul happened without conversion from sin because there was no sin. This grace was necessary for Adam and Eve to go to Heaven and also to experience the integrity of their forces around the whole desire of going to Heaven. In the case of the Apostles in the Upper Room, however, this grace required conversion from sin.

So, with sanctifying grace, Adam and Eve experienced a third kind of gift. These gifts from God to Adam and Eve were not supernatural—obviously, our community with the Holy Trinity is something completely above and beyond our nature, which is what the word "supernatural" means in this context—nor were they merely natural, because they couldn't be produced by our own human powers. Instead, they were gifts *beyond* nature designed to prepare us for the supernatural. In theological terms, these gifts are called *preternatural gifts* after two Latin words: *praeter*, "beyond," and *natura*, "nature." So, these preternatural gifts are "beyond but not above nature" and are characteristic of the state of Adam and Eve before the Original Sin.

Vatican II says that a human person is characterized by two things. The first is that no person may be an *object of use*, but every person must be a *subject of love*. Adam and Eve didn't use or abuse each other. Instead, they looked upon the presence of the other as an opportunity by which they could realize themselves in giving the gift of themselves. They showed integrity by their interest in the other. The second thing is that a human person only finds himself by *a sincere gift of himself to another.* Adam and Eve did not grasp to dominate each other. Adam and Eve did not take the gift of self from the other. They showed no power over the other. Instead, what they did was look on whatever power they had as a means to affirm the other and to give the gift of themselves to that other (cf. *Gaudium et Spes*, 25). This was due to a normal psychology at the basis of grace.

A True Gift Of Self

True human integrity finds itself not in what we can take, but instead in what we can give. True human integrity finds itself within; it doesn't have to be recognized by anybody else. It doesn't have to be written up in the newspaper or bring renown or fame. Instead, true human integrity involves the experience of the fullness of God within us and our desire to communicate that experience to the other. This is seen in Adam and Eve's first relationship, and it should be seen in every human relationship we experience in this world. Self-restraining love is the best symptom of normal human psychology. This is human nature as it ought to be.

Our experience of human nature is quite different. If we are honest with ourselves, we recognize that we are all born in this world with this fantastic powerful desire to take, to grasp, to get from the other, to try to still our desires. What must we do? We look on the other as the means on which we feed to get that integrity. This is not a result of the way we were created. It is a result of what we made ourselves in the first sin.

Adam and Eve, to persevere in the way they were created, had to continually rely on God, but preternatural and supernatural gifts are not something that man can produce by himself. Instead, in order to do this, he must fall constantly into the Everlasting Arms.

3

The Original Sin

The Way We Ought To Be

A normal human spirit is a spirit such as Adam and Eve had in their original creation. It is one in which their bodies were submitted to the practice of their souls; in which their passions, their emotions, were easily at the service of their reason and of their will; and in which their reason and their will—or their truth and their love—were easily at the service of God, in Whose grace they were created.

This is the way we ought to be. This is what it means to be a "normal human being." Because we have intelligence, it is impossible for us to be satisfied in the fullest sense of that word "happy" with anything less than seeing God "face to face" in Heaven, and we're preparing for that while we're here on earth. So, an engraced man is a human being as he ought to be. This is because he can arrive at the Beatific Vision.

None of us is born into this world this way. We are not born into the world the way we ought to be. Every single one of us is born into the world without being able to experience Divine intimacy in the here and now and thereby arrive at human perfection. As a result, the common human experience is not peace, but warfare within. This warfare is caused by the fact that we lost grace in the Original Sin.

The Original Sin was the first sin committed by Adam and Eve, which is described in Genesis as eating the fruit of a tree. Whatever was involved in this sin, it was an action that Adam and Eve undertook that went against the will of God. Adam and Eve were given a commandment—"You may freely eat of every tree of the garden; but of the tree of the knowledge of good and evil you shall not eat, for in the day that you eat of it you shall die" (Gen. 2:16-17). At the enticement of Satan—in this account, in the form of a serpent—they did not depend on God. Since this original integrity, this human wholeness, this normal man was a condition that they were created in, that could only be wrought and sustained by divine power since it was caused by the presence of grace. Adam and Eve, at every single moment of every single day, had to depend upon God in order to persevere in this condition. But, in this decision to go against God's instruction, they acted as though they could bring forth this beautiful integrity by their own power. In doing so, they did not depend on God to enlighten them and to guide them in this decision.

This showed little love. Adam and Eve acted as though they owned this condition, as though they did not receive it as a grace from the hands of a loving Creator. As a result, they lost grace. This is the way it's described in the book of Genesis: "Then the eyes of both were opened, and they knew that they were naked; and they sewed fig leaves together and made themselves aprons. And they heard the sound of the Lord God walking in the garden in the cool of the day, and the man and his wife hid themselves from the presence of the Lord God among the trees of the garden. But the Lord God called to the man, and said to him, 'Where are you?' And he said, 'I heard the sound of thee in the garden, and I was afraid, because I was naked; and I hid myself'" (Gen. 3:7-10).

In other words, the man is ashamed to be naked, even in the presence of the Creator. Why? Because he has lost grace. He cannot experience divine intimacy anymore. There is no vehicle, no means, no power in his soul to elevate him in order to be able to experience divine grace. From having been elevated to a condition in which their nature was sound because they experienced union with God through the supernatural gift of grace, by their sin Adam and Eve fell below nature.

Consequences of Sin

The Catholic Church has always taught that in the Original Sin we lost sanctifying grace; we lost divine intimacy. We also lost these marvelous gifts of grace that Adam and Eve received in their original creation that reflected sanctifying grace, the preternatural gifts. These gifts were present in Original Justice but lost in Original Sin. In the state of fallen yet redeemed nature we receive back grace but not these gifts. Our struggle to experience the perfect love of God is now a spiritual combat. However, it is with great hope because we struggle knowing that we are redeemed by God's love and grace.

- We lost infused knowledge; instead of this, the human race is now characterized by ignorance.

- We lost loving obedience; instead, we resent someone telling us what to do now and tend to want to dominate every situation. Life is not characterized now by cooperation in society; it is characterized by competition for domination. "Who will wear the crown?"

- Instead of a spontaneous virtue in which our passions easily went along with what we knew to be true, now our passions, like a warfare of spirit, tend to go their own way. In tending to go their own way, they tend not to be obedient to reason. Therefore, tendencies enter our soul in which we easily succumb to satisfying our feelings to the expense of what we know to be right.

Genesis describes how the Lord interrogates the people responsible for the sin. "Have you eaten of the tree of which I commanded you not to eat?" (Gen. 3:11) Then who did they blame? Did they accept responsibility? Do they blame themselves? No. The man says, "The woman whom thou gavest to be with me, she gave me fruit of the tree, and I ate" (Gen. 3:12). So, who does Adam blame? He blames God as well as Eve. "It was Your idea to put her here with me," he basically says. "She's the one that caused me to sin." Who does Eve blame? Does she accept responsibility? No. She blames the serpent. "The serpent beguiled me, and I ate" (Gen. 3:13). So, "passing the buck" is something that characterizes us even to this day.

Concupiscence

Then, as a result of losing grace, God enumerates the resultant punishments, which manifest in conditions in relationships that relate to abnormal psychology. "To the woman He says, 'I will greatly multiply your pain in childbearing and in pain you shall bring forth children. Yet your desire shall be for your husband and he shall rule over you'" (Gen. 3:16). The pain of childbirth is a result of the wounds of soul caused by our loss of grace. The life of woman, who ought to be in a natural relationship with her husband—comparable to that between a wise government and a free citizen—is now characterized by the desire to dominate her husband, almost through trickery: "Your desire shall be for your husband." Her husband dominates her by force. The word "desire" here has the flavor of an old Christian word, *concupiscence*, which means "a disordered desire." Now, instead of looking at her body as a means by which she can give the gift of herself to her husband, she looks upon her body as a possible occasion by which she can be dominated and manipulated against her will—which is what lust and concupiscence really means. Therefore, she covers her body with clothing to keep from being manipulated and dominated.

The man and the woman sew fig leaves together to cover their bodies. Is this because there is anything evil about their bodies—atoms and molecules, this flesh? No, it's because when they lost grace, the freedom and attitude of their spirits toward one another changed. This is seen in the fact that the woman now cannot freely give herself to the love of her husband because she fears that he will try to manipulate and dominate her.

We do not cover our bodies with clothes because they are wicked and evil. We cover our bodies with clothes because we experience what Pope St. John Paul II calls, in highly technical language, "the phenomenon of shame." Adam is ashamed at the presence of God. Why are we said to be ashamed at the presence of our naked bodies? They provide possible occasions by which we can be manipulated and dominated by another. Adam hides himself from God, naked and ashamed, because—in his opinion, since he lost grace and does not experience intimacy with God—he could be manipulated and dominated by God, Whom he looks upon now not as a loving Father, not as someone who gives the gift of Himself to him, but as a rival for power.

Disordered Desires

The reason that Adam and Eve sew the fig leaves together and hide their flesh isn't because the flesh in itself has anything sinful about it at all. God created the flesh. The reason they do this is because the flesh, because of all the goods and emotions connected with it, now has become a very powerful means by which human beings seek to show their power over one another. Remember, *no one may be an object of use; everyone should be a subject of love. A human being only finds himself by sincere gift of himself to another.* This is precisely what Adam and Eve are now not able to experience.

Everything becomes an occasion of power, even material wealth, which is connected to their bodies. Why do we have money? Why do we need possessions? We need these things so that we can survive in the face of our environment, so that we can have food to eat, so that our bodies can grow, so that our spirits might be free to pursue God. There is nothing evil about having wealth; the trouble is that now, after the Original Sin, we have a disordered desire and love of wealth. The love of money is the root of all evil in a disordered way, as though it alone could bring us happiness. But it is not the money itself; it's the power it can bring.

Even our good desires for perfection become an occasion for egotistical domination in pride. This is a great tragedy. Doing good becomes an occasion for evil.

The root and difficulty of all three of the areas where we as human beings experience problems as the result of the Original Sin—described by John in one of his letters as "the lust of the flesh and the lust of the eyes and the pride of life" (1 John 2:16)—is precisely the desire for power and domination. It is this which characterizes our need for the healing of the spirit.

Original Sin is the tragedy and shipwreck of the human race and its consequences. After Original Sin, we easily give in to our passions, which can cause egotistical pleasures to the expense of other people. This even affects the relationship between husband and wife. This is not what was willed by God, nor is it what is taught by Christianity, nor is it the way man was in the beginning.

Power is the real issue in lust, not feelings. We tend to give in to feelings through our egotistical pleasures, but we give in to these feelings because of our desire for power, just as greed for wealth results from a desire for power.

Our Power Struggle

The issue in all lust is possessiveness. There is nothing wrong with having money; the trouble is, we are enticed by money because we lost grace. We are enticed by money to make it into our god, as though it could bring us some sort of absolute power and authority over our lives, so that we need nothing and no one else, but instead that everyone needs us.

This possessiveness also characterizes the manipulation and domination that occurs in marriage as a result of the Original Sin. When man and women become naked and ashamed at the presence of their own naked bodies, it is because they do not wish to be manipulated and dominated by the other person. They do not wish to be an object of power. They no longer look at this body-soul composite as a means by which, through human sexuality, they can give the gift of themselves to one another. That self-giving would be expressed naturally in the donation that occurs in the physical act of giving life to children. Instead, they now look on the body as a means by which they can take from the other the satisfaction of their own passionate desires.

In other words, instead of saying, "It is good that you exist, because you come from the hands of the loving Creator," now human beings, as a result of the Original Sin, have a tendency to say, "It is good that you exist, because you make me feel good." That is the current basis for marriage. As soon as you don't make me feel good, the marriage ends. I don't have to suffer for you at all. Nor do I have to suffer any self-control, especially in my desire for you in our relationship.

This lack of God leads to a disorder not only within the individual or between the spouses—as in Adam's interior disquiet even in his own existence—but also between the rest of the family. When parents are in disorder, the kids also pick it up. This desire for competition and manipulation affects brothers. Cain slays Abel—practically the first brotherly act in the history of the human race, according to Genesis. Pope Benedict XVI has remarked along the lines that "some think we should have more fraternal authority in the Church," then quickly adds in humor, "but just look what the first two brothers did to each other." Family squabbles are the worst when brother hates brother.

Sin and its manipulative tendencies filter through the whole human race, until at the tower of Babel the very sign of our union as human beings—language, the sign of our rationality, the sign that should be the expression of our unity and communion as persons—becomes confused. And language itself becomes not an instrument of communication but of a lack of understanding. At Pentecost, when the Holy Spirit came upon the Apostles, they experienced a new language, a language of the Spirit that everyone could understand. Babel was reversed in Pentecost. The Holy Spirit was the means to heal this division among men because He healed the division in families, because He healed the division in the self. The Holy Spirit, Who brings grace, was brought to us by the Redeemer.

Grace Abounds More

Original Sin does end not in punishment. After the punishments for Original Sin are enumerated, God says to the serpent, "I will put enmity between you and the woman, and between your seed and her seed; he shall bruise your head, and you shall bruise his heel" (Gen. 3:15). At the beginning of time are the woman, the child, and the serpent; at the end of time, in the Book of Revelation, we have the woman, the child, and the dragon. All that occurs in Scripture between these two passages is the story of a struggle between the woman and the child against the serpent and the dragon. There is hope in this struggle given to Adam and Eve.

Why did God permit this Original Sin? Because He was to bring forth a greater grace to effect a healing of the human race—the grace of the Incarnate Word, the grace of the Second Person of the Trinity taking flesh so that He could die on the Cross to heal our spirits. Therefore, we have to say that normal psychology demands the presence of the Holy Spirit in man. Before the sin, man was joined to God in nature by grace; after the sin, he is joined to God in person by the miracle of the hypostatic union. Christ is our healer.

The healing of the spirit demands, first and foremost, a return to this Holy Spirit. The return to this Holy Spirit is only brought to us through the grace of Christ, who died on the Cross for us, experiencing suffering and death—two of our punishments for the Original Sin—so that He might truly bring back to us a new springtime of the spirit. This is a springtime into which we who had fallen down are elevated, through grace, to go to Heaven and to be healed in spirit.

4

Emotional Maturity

The important substructure that allows us to be open to the entrance of grace and a proper understanding and emotional appreciation of God is normal psychology. A normal psychology should lead us to emotional maturity, which is based in human integrity. Since the human soul is at the basis of all the various powers—nutritive, sensitive, and intellectual—integrity demands that all of these powers act in union. Indeed, these powers do influence each other through the human soul that is at their basis.

The nutritive powers are mere indicators of integrity and provide a physical basis for acting in integrity, but as such they are not the primary powers with which wholeness is concerned. The nutritive powers have no knowing and desiring life of their own, and so there cannot be a conflict between them and the higher part of the soul, nor can they resist the direction of the soul.

The sensitive powers of knowing and loving, on the other hand, must be properly formed in order for a man to be whole. This is not because they are the central forces that underlie wholeness but because the soul is one, and any movement in the higher part of the soul naturally includes them. The estimative or usefulness judgment must be properly formed, for example, for a person to carry out actions that contribute to wholeness. The passions in man have a two-pronged perfection: they are both oriented to particular good experiences, as are animal passions, and they are naturally born to be obedient to reason. The formation of both the estimative judgment and the passions, then, demands first an understanding of the truth about man. This includes all the powers present in human nature and their natural orientations both to their own goods and to the good of man as such.

Unfortunately, modern psychiatry does not recognize this basis of the human soul. Because of a lack of metaphysics, reason and intelligence are often looked on as the enemy of emotional integrity. Dr. Baars says: "Freud believed the repressing factor to be the superego, encompassing the conscience and thus also reason. As a result, *conscience and reason, being the alleged perpetrators* of so much untold neurotic suffering in the world, became increasingly suspect."

Catholic doctrine and Thomas Aquinas have always held that rather than be in *opposition* to emotional maturity, conscience and reason are the *basis* for emotional maturity. All the most important interior experiences of the integration of goods are caused by men understanding their nature and willing them as goods. For a complete experience of this, love in the emotional sense is most necessary. Emotional maturity is caused by spiritual maturity; this implies penetrating the emotional life with intellectual truth, thereby disposing emotional love and all its related passions to be supportive of the action of willed or volitional love. It is this union that finally makes human actions spontaneous in the full meaning of that word. Man wills the good he knows to be true not only with no *resistance* on the part of the passions, but also with the complete *support* of the passions. He then truly enjoys doing good.

"When the object of the sensory appetite is considered in the light of the universal, sensory life will in this respect come under the influence of reason and will more or less lose its egocentric character. Moreover, it will also desire the good of others. This results in a noticeable elevation of the emotional life in that it becomes more unselfish. ... [This is] true for all ... human emotions. Although they remain sensory appetites, they assume the highest and noblest human characteristics as a result of the natural influence of the intellectual appetite."

Though it is possible for human beings to control themselves using only willpower, or to do so for the satisfaction of one or the other of the emotional desires, this will not lead to full human integration. Full human integration only occurs when there are virtues introduced into the passions that make them easily moved according to the reasonable action of the will. Only then will the truth fill man and penetrate to the sense desires. The virtues involved in these desires are temperance in the pleasure appetite and fortitude in the irascible appetite.

Of course, man today does not experience this complete emotional maturity. This is caused by the Original Sin. The fault for this does not lie in the passions themselves, but in the loss of grace in the soul, which is primarily experienced as a weakness of will. There are two mistaken tendencies in reaction to this problem.

The first mistaken tendency is the idea that since the passions cause us to sin, the virtuous man must not have passions. This is a conclusion aided by an ancient philosophy called Stoicism, which taught that the passions were evil in themselves and were sicknesses of the soul. If one possessed the virtues of temperance and fortitude, one would have no objects in the passions. The obvious practical result of this philosophy is to meet one emotional experience with another. For example, when the sexual urge arises in puberty, it is often treated as evil in itself and met with either fear or energy, perhaps even efforts at suppressing the feeling from consciousness. If this is extreme, it becomes a repression. Thomas Aquinas is completely against this philosophy. He points out that one must control wicked passions that can lead us to sin, but that if one is motivated by justice in the will, for example, this justice will always overflow to the passions in an emotionally mature person. "Wherefore by reason of this kind of overflow, the more perfect a virtue is, the more passion it causes."

The second mistaken tendency is the already mentioned idea that reason is the enemy of integration because it comes completely from outside. This is the source of the feelgood mentality of today. The cure is to allow the unbridled experience of the passions with no concern from the conscience or reason. "The more they [the conscience and reason] fell into disrepute, the easier it became for unrestrained emotions to determine people's behavior. This is true for the emotions of love, fear, anxiety, worry, sadness, despair, and envy, and most of all, or course, for sexual feelings. No longer neurotically repressed or rationally restrained, which, we believe, contribute significantly to the increase of sexual promiscuity and unwanted pregnancies, the legal enactment of liberalized abortion laws, the almost contagious spread of the contraceptive mentality, the growing revenues from the pornographic trade, and the demands of 'modern man' for a 'new morality'".

What should be the proper model for emotional maturity? Dr. Baars uses the example of a girl riding a horse. The girl is the intellect and will, and the horse would be the passions. If the girl starves and beats the horse into submission, it will become extremely weakened, and when needed it may fail to carry the girl where she wants to go. It may even die and leave the girl on foot, which would make it much more difficult to go anywhere. On the other hand, if the girl gives the horse its head and just allows the horse to run free wildly wherever the horse wants to go, the two may fall over a cliff or into a ditch, and serious injury would be done to the girl.

If instead, the girl raises the horse and learns to both know the horse and to ride well, the girl and the horse act together almost as one. "Through trial and error, learning from mistakes and successes, final integration has been achieved. With continued good care of the horse by the woman the daily ride is pure joy. She is free to let her thoughts and memories go out to whatever she wants. All her energies become available for more important things in the deep satisfaction that she has become an expert horsewoman and free to go where she pleases because her horse serves her will."

So for Dr. Baars, the essence of spiritual maturity consists in virtue.

Fr. Charles Corcoran, O.P., expressed this attitude very well in his introduction to the English translation of *The Priest and the Sick in Mind*, by Anna Terruwe: "[...] virtue does not consist in sublimation [...] Rather does virtue consist in assumption, a process in which the higher agency takes up and transforms from within the lower powers, giving them a new intrinsic form and determination, moderating and changing them in a real physical way, giving them a coaptation and proportion to a higher end."

Though, in the final analysis, this can only be done by grace, reason can and should prepare the way. When passions are irrationally formed, reason cannot enter them; and though a person can certainly experience grace in this formation, real integrity—and, therefore, joy in the truth—will escape them.

Disruption Of The Passions

So far we have discussed the difficulties caused by the Original Sin, the original tragedy in the human race experience—how we lost sanctifying grace, the supernatural gift of grace and the preternatural gifts, which led to our desires for manipulation and domination.

Although we lost these supernatural and preternatural gifts, we did not lose the natural gifts. That is why Catholics don't believe that man, by nature, is completely depraved. Instead, we believe that the natural gifts—the intellect, the will, the passions, and the body—all remain in their natural tendencies for their particular goods. The intellect remains oriented toward truth; the will remains oriented toward good; the passions remain in their natural orientation of obedience to the intellect, to truth, and to the will. The body, of course, has its natural tendency toward death and suffering.

The difficulty is that without grace, without the ordering of God, these things cannot be brought together completely. As a result, we experience not just moral evil—this domination we addressed in the last chapter—but also a kind of disruption in our passions, akin to how we experience physical illness.

Physical illness, in some sense, is a result of sin because it is a consequence of the Original Sin, but nobody is morally responsible for physical illness in itself. However, psychological difficulties are a different matter. Soviet philosopher Solzhenitsyn once wrote: "I insist that the problems of the west are not political; they are psychological and moral. When dissatisfaction with government is expressed, it should be understood not in terms of political failure but of weakened religious and ethical foundations in modern society. A problem like inflation in the midst of plenty is a psychological and morale problem. I am convinced that the only salvation for the East and the West lies in a moral and psychological rebirth."

The Re-Ordering of Truth

Psychological healing is a big issue today. Before the 1960s, we weren't supposed to have any passions in Catholicism—this was not actually true, but unfortunately people popularly thought it to be the case—rather, we were supposed to be stoics. After the 1960s, we discovered feelings and passions, and now everything is feelings, as in "wo, wo, wo, wo, feelings. How could it be so wrong, when it feels so right?"

Properly ordered passions or feelings are necessary parts of developing emotional maturity. Today we experience a lot of problems with people who have disordered feelings within. These disordered feelings do not just lead them to sin, nor do they simply create morale problems. These disordered feelings result from their inability, almost like a sickness, to carry out or change their orientation by their wills. They have fixations on things, for example, or perhaps they don't feel loved.

Sigmund Freud believed that the origin of emotional problems, which has become especially prevalent in our materialist culture, had to do with a conflict between our emotions or our passions and our rationality, the law, the truth. He had a very peculiar idea of the law or the truth, an idea that came from a nineteenth-century philosopher named Immanuel Kant. Kant believed that the truth and the law were absolutes that flowed from within, from one's need, and there was no way to investigate them objectively. One could not decide whether one law could be played off against another or whether one was more important than another; all were absolute completely, and there was no recourse to discovering why they were absolute or whether one could be abrogated in a given situation. This is because Kant reformed truth. Before Kant, truth was *the correspondence of the mind to the thing*; after Kant truth became *the correspondence of the thing to the mind.* Truth was completely subjective and changed from person to person.

When applied to law, this meant that there was no origin of law within the human subject determined by his objective nature. Law was merely an imposition from outside the person on man's freedom. Power created law. Since there was no natural law, there could be no mitigation or interpretation of law from discovery of the spirit over the letter.

The classic example of this is seen in *Les Miserables.* Inspector Javert will uphold the law in the face of a poor man who is almost innocent and was sent to the galleys for twenty years for stealing a loaf of bread because he and his children were starving. It is silly "justice," in a way, but the law was the law, property rights were absolute, everything was absolute. There was no recourse, no mitigation, nothing whatsoever. It was this philosophy of law that Freud was dealing with. He rightly though such an interpretation of law caused emotional illness.

True Emotional Conflict

Freud believed that the true conflict was caused by this super-arching experience of what people expected of you versus what you should feel. The problem, therefore, is that the whole purpose of the cure of that part of the human spirit, which has to do with emotional illness, was freedom from the law.

In Catholicism, we do not believe this. We believe the passions have a natural connection to obedience of reason and will, and you can find this teaching in the *Catechism of the Catholic Church.* Obedience to reason and will doesn't destroy our passions or cause us to become neurotic. Let's say I have an inordinate attachment for a particular woman, and this attachment is leading me to erotic feelings for her that I wish to carry out in erotic acts. If I deny myself these acts because I know that I'm not married to this woman and therefore that it is evil to act out these feelings, I don't thereby create a complex in myself. What happens is that there is a remitted good—namely, the satisfaction of my feelings—but because I have affirmed a deeper good—namely, the rights of this person and the rights of the situation—I have created emotional maturity in myself through self-control. In other words, if there is a psychological problem in a person, truth does not cause it, but rather it is caused by a person's failure to submit his or her feelings to the truth. There is something within the person that does not allow his or her feelings to submit to the control of reason and will. They are "out of control" is one way to put it.

Baars sums up this position thusly: "The classic Freud interpretation of emotional illness is a conflict between reason and the passions." There here are two basic desires in the passions. The one has to do with the good in itself—love, hate, desire, aversion, joy, sorrow; the other has to do with the good as something useful—hope, despair, courage, fear, and anger. The natural order among these two experiences of the emotions is that we first experience our emotions toward something as desirable in itself, as good in itself, as created the way it was created by God. We seek to be present to something as God is present to it. The second experience is that we approach it as useful or harmful, as something that helps us or harms us.

The trouble is that because of the lack of morals education or because of poor morals education, we have reversed this order. Not only that, but people sometimes experience something as harmful or useful before they can experience it as good or evil in itself, and so their whole experience of something as good or evil becomes colored by their experience of it as harmful or useful. Healing of the spirit on the level of nature is accomplished in psychological healing. Freud's clinical work was brilliant, but his explanation of therapy, cure, or healing was flawed because he had a flawed picture of the human soul—a Kantian idea of the soul. The soul must include the intellect and will. Much of neurotic behavior, which seems so irrational, comes from a lack of proper foundation in sense knowledge for the union with the intellect and will. This is especially true of the estimative sense. There is an estimative sense in animals, where the lamb sees the wolf and escapes, for example. This is caused by the fact that the lamb has an emotional experience of the wolf as harmful to him. The lamb is not taught that, but it runs away.

In men, it's different: this emotional experience has to be caused by education, because we're such variable creatures, and we have almost an infinity open to us through our spirits, our intellects, and our wills. This means that sometimes, through bad morals education, people receive the impression that something is harmful and to be feared when in itself it is actually good. As a result, the whole experience of fear or striving—what we would call courage—colors our judgment, so that instead of being allowed to experience the goodness of something in itself, we can only experience something as useful to us. Either we have to conquer it, or it has to help us in some way before we can love it. If we fail to conquer it, then self-restraining love goes out the window.

Effects of Bad Morals Education

Would you like to be loved by your friends only as long as you are useful to them? When you are no longer useful, in a sense, the love ends. This is what materialism and denial of spirit causes.

The whole of western culture has become this way because of a very peculiar bad morals education.

Bad morals education can easily lead people to an emotional conflict, an excessive fear. Suppose a child, when they reach puberty, is taught that the feelings or the emotions that arise in us that pertain to our sexuality are evil. It's true, such feelings can often lead us to sin, but they're not evil in themselves. Who created the passions? Who made sexuality feel good? God created the passions. In themselves, they cannot be evil.

Sister Wendy Beckett, the late BBC television personality and art historian, once had a discussion with Bill Moyers, who asked her, "Sister Wendy, all these paintings are filled with naked bodies. Doesn't that upset you?" And she said, "Well no, Bill, it doesn't upset me at all." And he asked, "Why not?" And she said, "Well, Bill, God made the body, and He didn't make any mistakes."

The problem isn't the body or the feelings. It's what we make of them. But suppose a child, either through experience or through instruction, comes to believe that all experiences of a particular kind are evil. As soon as these emotions arise in them, they experience fear at their presence, as though they are harmful in themselves. The realistic way of coming to deal with these emotions is for the adolescent to say, "Okay, I feel these things. They're driving me toward a physical attraction with another human being, but there are certain ways I can express this that are appropriate and certain ways that aren't," and then to submit to the guidance of adults. Instead of exploring this slowly—in other words, loving the idea of being able to experience the gift of yourself, first through your soul and then through your body, eventually to be completed in marriage as adults—the whole thing becomes a matter of fear to the adolescent. If it is deep enough, if his or her personality is formed enough, the fear could be so

St. Thomas Aquinas Rescues Modern Psychology

strong that the adolescent could blot out the whole experience of sexual feelings altogether and not even admit to them in his or her consciousness.

Passion Versus Responsibility

The trouble is that all our passions have a natural tendency to be obedient to reason. Passion is like a strong movement toward something, and if reason and will have not been brought in to humanize it, it doesn't go away. It's always there underneath. Since reason and will aren't giving it peace through choice, passion breaks out against our choice when we least expect it, often in spectacular and strange ways.

Virtuous persons, when they integrate their sexuality within, experience the virtues of temperance. They enjoy this. They're happy about it, because it doesn't create tension in them. But in a person who either experienced control or lack of self-control through suppressing the passion not from true informed choice but merely from unrealistic fear, there is no realistic control in this. There is constant tension, and very strange things happen almost against the person's will. Passion jumps out contrary to our desires. This person needs healing.

But where has the conflict occurred? Is it between the real truth and the passion? It is between the positive passion present toward the good itself and the experience that we have in our passions of usefulness and harmfulness. For example, fear can block out love. It can seek to bury authentic love alive and not allow it to enter into the higher part of ourselves, where it can be governed and controlled in a virtuous way by our reason and will. This is the origin of psychological conflict: a person becomes neurotic because they have this unreasoning fear that never allows this tendency to submit to the guiding control of reason and will.

58

What is the proper procedure to help someone heal from this conflict? Tell them untruths? Tell them to practice illicit sexual conduct in order to solve their problems? No, that is false. Should we tell them falsehoods about Catholic doctrine? No, that is also false. They must have a realistic explanation of morality according to the truth so that they might become free again and truly submit their conflicts to the control of intellect and will.

Instead, what we've done in our culture excessively is to do away with responsibility with regard to almost anything. People do not face consequences of any kind for their actions. Two of the big contributing factors for this development have been contraception, which looks upon as a child as merely useful or harmful, and divorce, which looks upon the marriage bond (or any promise, really) as breakable, even when it leads to the dissolution of the family.

Dr. Baars once related his experience dealing with the shortage of food in a concentration camp to the origin of the philosophy of contraception:

Once on the battlefields of WWI, now in the concentration camps of WWII, France paid its price for taking the lead in one of the most successful campaigns in modern history—some 120 years earlier the campaign of birth control. Successful their campaign had been because birth control appealed so much to the selfish element in every human being. It eliminates the responsibilities and duties of love. It decries the consequences of romance. And it educates young people in their selfish desires, interests, and in the indulgence of their selfish pleasures. In destroying the morality of its youth—and I would say this is true of some of our culture today—this led the way to the destruction of its own existence. For it removed in its children the backbone of perseverance against evil. They had nobody to blame but themselves because they were only supporting Malthus' Theory that the mad rabbit-like multiplication of the members of the human race would cause a disaster and exhaustion of the world's food supply.[6]

This same philosophy affects the abortion culture. Behind the abortion mentality is the question of bearing children in terms of whether a child fits into my life or not. That same question is behind the contraceptive mentality. "I will not have a child because it isn't useful to me. It does not fit into my life." This creates the idea that people are lovable only as long as they're useful. In other words, the useful, in its emotions, comes first. All our loves and hates become formed based not on what's really good or what's really evil, or the way God created the world, but rather by what's harmful or useful to me. In normal psychology, the opposite is true. I first love something as good, then it becomes useful to me. When use comes first, then my needs or my truth become the standard for judging reality and all truth. What can result from this but egotism of the spirit?

Healing Through Loving Assumption

Egotism of the spirit is never liberating because, again, *no person may be a subject of use. Every person must be a subject of love. A person can only find himself in a sincere gift of himself to another.* One thing that lust leads to is the tendency to not give yourself to another, but rather to look upon others as persons to take from for your own perceived good. Emotions can't be formed properly this way: they must start out with the good in itself, then go to what is helpful

[6] Conrad Baars, *Doctor*, 110.

and harmful to me in light of that good, then back to the good in itself. If there is no good in itself, then people seek to satisfy themselves by their own egotism. When they do that, their emotions become seriously compromised along with their moral life.

But the healing of the spirit that involves psychological difficulties requires the liberation of these passions that have been buried alive. These passions must again be submitted to the control of the intellect and will. The truth must enter into this. A realistic morals explanation of the Ten Commandments is absolutely necessary in this context in order to allow the person the freedom to release these passions so that then they can be guided again. The problem is not the body, the passions, sexuality, money, or any of those things in themselves. The problem is our use of them and the fact that perhaps we've been wrongly educated in what they involve. To experience healing of the spirit, the ego must be opened again to the control of intelligence.

5

The Types of Emotional Illness

The Psychopathic Personality and Religion

One of the signs of emotional maturity is the ability to experience guilt at the perception of wrongdoing. Many modern psychologists would maintain that feelings of guilt are rarely the sign of a healthy personality. Yet, if the perspective of emotional maturity presented by Dr. Baars is accurate, guilt would be indicated psychologically when the person truly perceives in their conscience that they have done wrong. "There will be a defect in the psychic life if a sense appetite acts contrary to reason. This is not a defect as regards the sensory inclination itself, however, because the particular appetite will become quiescent once its goal has been attained. But it is a defect in the relationship of appetite to reason, which is experienced as a feeling of discomfort and uneasiness. Hence, it is more than an intellectual awareness of the wrong that has been done; it is an actual feeling of incompleteness. This is the way in which well-balanced, mature individuals spontaneously react and it forms the basis of the *feeling of guilt* which results from performing acts that are morally wrong. It is an experience of the psychological incompleteness of the human act."

This is the case in a really mature person. There would be the two contraries to this in human experiences of guilt: when one

63

feels guilty when having done nothing or next to nothing wrong, and when one does *not* feel guilty when one has done a serious wrong. The latter experience is characteristic of the psychopathic personality, a personality type which priests and religious sometimes encounter in pastoral care and spiritual direction.

Psychopathic Types

Dr. Baars agrees with his colleague Dr. Terruwe that this personality type is constitutionally determined, as opposed to neurotics who suffer from a personality disorder that is situationally determined. The psychopath, then, may not recover from his abnormality, but with grace and understanding he can learn to control it. Dr. Terruwe gives a much more detailed analysis of this personality type in her book translated by Dr. Baars, *The Priest and the Sick in Mind*, and so I will refer to her examination.

First, in psychopaths, "the subordination of appetites to reason will be greatly diminished or completely lacking, depending upon the degree of impairment." Since they have no ability to relate the life of reason to the life of the concrete everyday experience, they are almost completely lacking in feelings of guilt. Though each psychopath, like each person, is unique, one can distinguish groups who manifest this "diminished control of the emotional life by the intellect resulting from constitutional factors." According to Dr. Terruwe, they are: the *hysterical psychopath*, the *fantastic liar* or *pathological liar*, the *amoral/asocial type*, the *hypomaniac*, and the *sexual psychopath*. Spiritual advisers must be aware of each of these.

The hysterical psychopath

The hysterical psychopath is the most important for spiritual advisers. The hysterical psychopath is "dominated by a morbid urge to attract the attention of others." This is due to a deficiency of feeling. These people are unable to satisfy their need for rapport with others in a natural way, so they do it in an unnatural way. They do this to only satisfy their usefulness desires. They cannot experience true friendship because everyone is an object of use to them, and so they are insincere. This person seeks to "create situations in which they feel they can mean something to others." They may be the imagined invalid or the "eternally misunderstood individual." Regarding priests and religious, they have a disturbing tendency to imagine they are enjoying supernatural favors. Dr. Terruwe writes: "It would be most desirable if a book were written about the relations between supernatural graces and abnormal mental states."

Dr. Terruwe gives a famous example from the autobiography of Teresa of Avila regarding Magdalen of the Cross, a false Franciscan nun and mystic who threw all of Spain into religious fervor by her ecstasies. Magdalen later publicly confessed that her ecstasies were false and did penance to the Inquisition to delight in all the attention paid to her. This unhealthy desire to draw attention can even lead to slanderous accusations against priests or religious.

The pathological liar

The second is the pathological liar. These imagine and tell the most fantastic stories. Priests and religious are often victimized by these sorts of individuals who may actually believe what they imagine to be true. "The activity of man's imagination is strongly influenced by his emotions, and when these emotions are not penetrated and governed by reason, as is true in psychopathic personalities, naturally the result is that the imagination, too, will function in an uncontrolled manner."

The amoral psychopath

Amoral psychopaths find "feelings of charity and devotion, as well as ethical and religious feelings [...] foreign to them." They may even become callous criminals because they enjoy the evil they do. Everything they do, even actions like Holy Communion, they do to satisfy their own selfish feelings. They may not be morally culpable for this, but others must be protected from them.

The hypomaniac

The hypomaniac has an atrophy of the "passion of hope." For hypomaniacs, risk and restraint in activities do not exist. In the priest this may take the form of boring his congregation with interminable sermons without the slightest appreciation for the effect of his sermons on them. For the laity, this may take the form of constantly thinking up fantastic and unreasonable schemes which do not have a prayer of practical success and disappointment if the priest fails to implement them.

The sexual psychopath

The sexual psychopath is especially important today. These individuals have an abnormal need for sexual gratification. A good example is Messalina, the wife of the Roman emperor Claudius. Claudius supplied her with a brothel to satisfy her sexual desire. This abnormal desire may be realized in many forms of extreme sexual behavior: homosexuality, narcissism, sadism, masochism, fetishism, pedophilia, etc. These same acts may be done by normal people, but those who suffer from the psychopathic personality are especially prone to them.

Spiritual Direction of Psychopaths

What would be the principles for the guidance of psychopathic personalities? The spiritual director must realize that the inability of the psychopath to guide himself is not his fault since it is constitutionally determined. He cannot help himself. "An uncontrolled emotional life is a tremendously heavy burden for man, but whoever bears this cross with a will which is properly directed through grace bears it through Christ and Christ bears it with him." The director or superior must tolerate the psychopath with patience. But it would not be correct to just leave the person to his fate. The first key to dealing with this person is rationality. Since he cannot guide his emotions by reason, the director or superior must do it for him. The psychopath will normally not be responsive to this direction, but "the director must stand his ground and calmly assert his will." If the psychopath will not follow direction, then he must be left to act out on his inclinations, but not saved from the consequences. Since psychopaths only respond to the concrete, the consequences: loss of health, honor, respect, affection, and the like may teach him a lesson. To just allow the psychopath to act with no guidance is the worst thing.

The second key to guidance is genuine affection. The purpose of guidance should not just be to save the community money or embarrassment, but a genuine desire for the good of the wounded individual. "If guidance is to have any measure of success, the psychopaths have to sense that he who advises and guides them has only the best intentions and honestly and sincerely desires their well-being."

There are two final points that are imperative. The first is that the community must normally support superiors dealing with psychopaths. People with emotional dysfunctions who possess little or no rationality and who are eager to stand out delight in using members of the community to free them from confronting their own weakness. As long as they can find just one member who will do this, they have an ally to keep them from guidance. This is disastrous to the psychopath, to the community and to the superior. Affection can never lead one to sacrifice truth to spare a person's feelings.

Second, Dr. Terruwe warns priests to be especially wary of women psychopaths. Since the twin qualities needed to guide them are rationality and affection, this presents special problems for a man seeking to guide women. Dr. Terruwe points out that many women will "leave no stone unturned to try to make the director change his decision." This includes trying to dominate the director emotionally. She advises the priest to remain calm and to simply seek to speak the truth. If he once gives in to the temptation to try to counter the opposition of the psychopath emotionally, then he is lost. Dr. Terruwe clearly states: "As soon as he allows himself to be dominated by his emotions, however slightly, his position will be weakened, because few men are a match for women as far as emotions are concerned."

Origins of Neurosis

Neurotic behavior is an acquired emotional difficulty—as opposed to psychopathic behavior, which is constitutionally determined. For Dr. Baars, there are two main types of neurosis: *repression* and *affirmation*. The classic neurosis is the repressive type, and since this is the one most psychiatrists are familiar with, it is important to treat it first. Dr. Baars defines repression as: "an emotion which arises in the psyche and a force which opposes and represses this emotion." This opposition does not resolve the emotional drive or cause it to disappear but rather buries it alive. The emotion continues to influence the life of the soul, but from a subconscious perspective. The outward signs of this influence become pathological.

Dr. Baars is of the opinion that the source of the conflict cannot be the conscience and the moral law (*superego*) as Freud believed because for one thing the objects of the good are different when viewed from the point of view of the intellect and the senses. "Properly speaking, a conflict results when two opposing emotions are present simultaneously in regard to one and the same object.... To speak of a conflict it is necessary that two or more appetites are aroused by the same object. In this way each appetite will respond to the object in a different way."

There are two possible sources of conflict between powers of desire, as is clear from the treatment of normal psychology. One is a conflict between the will and the passions, while the other is a conflict within the passions themselves. Since the passions are naturally born to be obedient to reason, there can be no unnatural conflict between the will and the passions. A diabetic may find candy sweet to the pleasure principle, but his reason and will tell him he must deny himself this pleasure. An amputee may find surgery repulsive because of the pain and the assault on his body, yet if this is the only way to save his life, he will choose to embrace it because of his health. A man may desire sexual pleasure because it feels good, but he may choose to deny himself this feeling because it is evil.

Freud thought this last denial was the source of repression, but in fact this denial is a sign and an origin of emotional maturity. In this denial, reason penetrates more into the life of the passions, especially for those of us wounded by Original Sin. In other words, the more the natural law and authentic human reason guide emotional development, the more human the person experiencing this will become, even when this leads to denial of the passions. The universal truth about man will influence the usefulness judgment, which guides and directs the sensitive life, and true integration will occur.

The problem is that moral norms can be interpreted only in a sensory and non-intellectual way. Children do this because they do not have developed intellects, but this is not normal in adults.

To base something like obedience only on fear of the superior's reaction or pleasure at accomplishing things may be normal in children, but it in no way arrives at the maturity envisioned in the vow of obedience.

As long as the usefulness judgment is correctly formed, then all is well. "Because of a misinformed usefulness judgment, it is possible for man to consider a desire for a pleasurable object as harmful, and thus to arouse in the utility appetite (irascible appetite), for instance, the emotion of fear. In the cause of conflict between the emotions of these two appetites—desire and fear—the sensory life does not possess any natural means of solution." This is the second possible conflict between the two emotional appetites (pleasure or concupiscible, and utility or irascible) and is the origin of neurotic behavior.

The Sexual Urge and Repression

For example, the sexual urge always arises in puberty. God himself made the pleasures in this regard. Pope St. John Paul II taught that this is the first emotional experience a child has in which the world moves beyond self-gratification to being other-centered. Granted, it is only on the sensory level and very imperfect. Still, the sexual urge contains the seeds of what will eventually grow into the mature commitment of marriage in a mature person. Moreover, the pleasures are so great here because the goods of fidelity, fecundity, and friendship are so important for human development.

Suppose a child has received the impression from well-meaning educators who want him to avoid sin that all the pleasures connected with sexuality are sinful in themselves. There was a Puritanical strain in Christianity in which it was taught that the pleasures in marriage are tolerated evils because of the good of bearing children. So when the passion or pleasure arises, the child—from the emotion of fear—opposes the very feeling itself. A conflict therefore occurs not among the intellect and the will and the passions, but within the passions themselves. It is a conflict caused not by moral teaching, but by *bad* moral teaching. In fact, since God made the pleasures, they cannot be evil in themselves.

Normally, if any emotional urge like this were subject to the control of intellect and will, continual denial over time would lead to the "*formation of a habit,* so that the urge would respond to the guidance of reason with increasing facility." In this abnormal control, reason and will are increasingly left out of the picture as well as from the behavior that results from this control because the repressing passion will not allow the existence of the repressed feeling to enter into the arena of control. One emotion is used to control another, rather than the intellect and will controlling the emotion. One does not experience peace and facility in control, but instead one experiences a complete lack of control and tension. For example, one hates the idea of sexual passion, but has a compulsive desire to look at pornography on the internet. "To put it differently, the repressing emotion has been *wedged* between the repressed emotion and reason. Thus, the action of the repressed emotion remains outside the control of reason and will. Only when the repressing emotion recedes and normal psychological conditions return, will guidance by reason become a possibility."

Depending on the intensity of the repressing emotion, the repressed emotion may be more or less admitted into consciousness. Dr. Baars makes an important distinction for all moral theology: consciousness of the influence of the passion is not the same as willing it. Will demands the application of reason to the passion. "An emotional arousal may be present more or less consciously even when it is not voluntary." Thomas Aquinas makes the point also regarding things like temptation and the sin of morose delectation, which is sin in engaging or failing to drive away thoughts regarding pleasure. "Delectation is said to be morose not from a delay of time, but because reason in deliberating dwells thereon, and fails to drive it away."

Several important factors must be observed in this conflict. The repressing emotion may attack the repressed emotion during every stage of the expression of the emotion—love, desire, or joy; hate, aversion, or sorrow. The emotional conflict can also involve emotions in the same appetite. For example, one can repress fear by renewed fear, or fear by anger, or anger by fear. Many people today have the impression that even the feeling of anger is always sinful, despite the fact that the Lord Jesus became angry and even Scripture teaches, "Be angry and do not sin" (Eph. 4:26). Anger is one of the passions and must be felt, especially to defend one from evil in the face of a sinful world. There is a distinction between feeling anger and its expression—for example, tantrums or losing one's temper. Yet, many educators do not make that distinction.

Repression and Temperament

Another important factor in repression is that the nature of the repressing emotion often depends on the temperament of the person suffering from it. In people with a dominant personality, the character may be dominated by emotional energy or courage. One puts accomplishing things in the place of any real experience of loving and being loved. In one with a weak personality, fear may be the predominant experience of the psyche. This is important for distinguishing kinds and guidance in repression. Freud thought repression was basically about sexuality, but it can actually be about almost any emotional experience.

One final point regards the order of the appetites. In normal emotional integration, the pleasure appetite comes first. Love is the predominant emotion because it expresses union with the goodness of being as such. The usefulness emotions only enter when love or hate are frustrated by difficulty in obtaining their objects. In repression, the utility appetite is predominant, and so all goods are judged according to their usefulness or harmfulness but nothing is really good in itself. This is contrary to nature and produces a utilitarian spirit and tension. It is contrary to the personalistic norm of Vatican II which states that *no person may be an object of use, every person must be a subject of love.* From this point of view everything, even God is loved only as a useful good.

Priest and religious must apply these ideas judiciously, especially regarding vocations and people in formation. Some women enter convents from fear of men. Some men become priests because they want to be loved and taken care of. They fear the normal demands of adult life. These are emotions controlling very spiritual decisions, and they are inadequate. Basic moral maturity is necessary for anyone pursuing a religious vocation of whatever kind. This can only result from a free and informed choice in a person with basic emotional maturity.

Types of Repression

There are two kinds of repression: the *hysterical* and the *obsessive-compulsive.* They are distinguished by personality type and by which predominates, the repressing or repressed emotion in the soul.

After repression occurs, the repressing emotion may allow the repressed emotion to do as it pleases. In this case the repressed emotion becomes more pronounced in the character. This is the hysterical neurosis. On the other hand, the repressing emotion may be more dominant. This is the obsessive-compulsive neurosis. The distinction is important because they truly involve different sorts of personalities and also different guidance on the part of the therapist or confessor.

The hysterical neurosis

In the hysterical neurosis, the repressed emotion is allowed to go as it pleases and is not under the control of the intellect and will. Persons who suffer from this repression are unaware that their emotional attitude—and, often, their behavior—are pathological. They have no self-knowledge and very little insight into their condition. The uncontrolled nature of the repressed emotion can show itself in many ways, from hypersensitivity and a pathological need to be recognized in one who has repressed the assertiveness emotions, to uncontrolled sexual behavior in one who is afraid of the whole idea of sexuality, to physical paralysis. The latter is the result of what is known as conversion reaction. "Conversions may affect every area of the sensory life: the sensibility, the voluntary motor system, the external senses, the vaso-vegetative system, the consciousness, and others. No matter where they become manifest, neither reason nor the repressing emotion has any influence over them." For example, a person suffering from repressed fear may become paralyzed.

Dr. Baars is of the opinion that this neurosis is due to a lack of influence of the intellect on the emotional life. If the intellect were more apparent in this neurosis, the repressed emotion would not be so free. He maintains that in his experience people who suffer from hysterical neurosis often do not have an acute intelligence, although this is not without exception.

The obsessive-compulsive neurosis

The obsessive-compulsive neurosis has a different cause because there the repressing emotion is much more evident. The repressed emotion has little influence in this neurosis. Generally, Dr. Baars divides this neurosis into three types, each determined by which of the repressing emotions is most evident: fear (also called anxiety), energy (courage, in the Scholastic sense) and a combination of fear camouflaged by energy.

Repressive neuroses are acquired and not innate, and so they may develop even in normal and healthy children under the right circumstances. In the fear neurosis, for example, fear can show itself in somatic signs, like tremors and shivering, or in psychic signs. One can be excessively fearful of making bad confessions even though one's sins are only venial or when there is no sin at all. There are many similarities between this sort of person and the person with the scrupulous conscience.

This unreasoning fear is not only seen in strange reactions. The whole of life is penetrated by fear, including the imagination. These emotions may show themselves powerfully in dreams. A person with the fear neurosis may also have strange and powerful phobias to things, persons, or circumstances of life. Sometimes these fears may turn to anger, which demonstrates that the person is trying to resist the fear. When the fear cannot be resisted any longer, then the person has states of depression. The opposite of this is the energy neurosis. Not every overachiever is an energy neurotic, but one who has an energy neurosis is excessively assertive and domineering. "If this ambitious attitude is not directed at external objects, but at emotions and feelings, this driving force will also take a prominent place in the clinically observable psychic manifestations. The undesirable emotions will be radically repressed, so effectively in fact that the victor seems to be a balanced person."

Though this masks as reasonable self-control, it is not. An energy neurotic's whole life is characterized not by inner peace, but by inner restraint and coldness. Though one is efficient, there is no natural warmth in relationships. "Tenderness and compassion disappear," especially in women. A man or woman may outwardly appear a great success, but all of their relationships are only superficial. They are unable to experience the true empathy symptomatic of a virtuous life. Religion should not make people cold and tense. Nor should morality do so. "[T]heir self-restraint is nothing but a forcing back, a certain attitude imposed from the outside."

Each of these forms of neurosis has physical manifestations that are very important in distinguishing them. Only a trained psychiatrist who is a medical doctor should undertake to diagnose them. Symptoms such as decreased or absent muscle-stretch reflexes and systolic and dystolic blood pressure as well as blood sugar levels are important indicators. Again, this is because of the unity of the human soul.

The third type of neurosis, fear camouflaged by energy, is a sort of double repression. First, pleasure is repressed by fear, and then fear by energy. The difference between this type of neurotic and the ordinary energy neurotic is that this person has a great desire to achieve, but his fear affects his effective pursuit of this desire. This type of fear neurotic is more intelligent, and the passions are more subject to reason here. But the same condition is generally present as in all the others: the emotional life cannot be controlled and directed by the intellect and will.

Pseudoneurotic reactions

There is one last point that is important for religious. Dr. Baars identifies what he calls "*pseudoneurotic reactions.*" These are emotional reactions and strange behaviors which are caused by a passing situation and not by a deep-seated emotional conflict. The person is otherwise completely normal except for the emotionally troubling situation. Dr. Baars gives the example of a woman who suffered great fatigue and irritability because she was living over a carpenter's shop that had a buzzsaw. She wanted to move. In the course of therapy, Dr. Baars understood the woman was practicing birth control through sexual withdrawal. He explained the psychological harm of this practice because of the frustration of the purposes of the act and the true natural ends to which it is oriented. When she began to practice natural family planning, the situation changed, and her problem disappeared. She now enjoyed living over the carpenter's shop.

Different Therapeutic Methods

The therapy for each of these neuroses is different because the conditions are different. The most important aspect of therapy for hysterical neurosis, for example, is to bring the repressed emotion into consciousness because the person is largely unaware of the tension that exists in this regard. The classic *psychoanalytic* method of Freud seems indicated here. Once this occurs, cure can only be accomplished when the cause of the excessive passions is identified. This includes a proper moral education to substitute for the bad one received. One may do this "by eliminating an external cause, by removing ignorance, by substituting correct insights for erroneous ones, and by helping the patient to see things in their true light and to appreciate their true value."

Therapy for obsessive compulsive neurosis is very different. To attempt to force the repressed emotion back into consciousness by a method such as psychoanalysis would only increase the illness because it would increase the action of the repressing emotion. Psychoanalysis is not indicated here. In each instance, the therapy for this neurosis is somewhat distinct but oriented to the same goal.

In the fear neurosis, trust is the key. The therapist does not have to worry about transference here, as trust in the therapist is key so that the fear can diminish. "This necessary feeling of confidence presupposes the presence of two conditions in the patient: first, trust that the therapist's understanding of emotional disorders and their related moral aspects is correct; and second, confidence in him as a person." For a Christian, this indicates that the patient must have confidence that the therapist has a true understanding of the teaching of the Church on morals. This must be coupled with an almost intuitive trust that the therapist has a sincere affection for him as an individual and is interested in his good.

The therapy for the energy neurotic is based on the contrast between the two types of personality. Here the utility appetite is out of all bounds. So, therapy demands that one must try to diminish and end the excessive energy, but also try to restore the repressed emotions to their natural place. This is very hard for the energy neurotic because he is convinced that his way of life is ideal. "*Rest* is one of the first things that the therapist should prescribe for the energy neurotic."

The person's lack of rest can be caused by his willed determination to succeed in whatever he wants. These people are so successful that only a complete psychological collapse will convince them there is anything wrong. If the energy neurosis is determined by the intellect—which is the case when the person is intellectually convinced that it is his moral duty to suppress his feelings—then a good explanation of surrender to God by imperfect man is needed.

The most important thing is not to make a threatening demand that these people understand what is happening to them, but rather to undertake a gradual and spontaneous process whereby the hypertrophied emotion can be reduced and the repressed emotion can again be assimilated into the higher self.

The therapy for fear camouflaged by energy is also based on a flawless explanation of the philosophy of man and the place of the emotions therein. Both Catholic doctrine in general and Thomistic philosophy in particular are especially helpful.

The Necessity Of Trust

Psychological healing does not, in itself, relate to morals. Psycho-logical illness is almost like a physical illness, but it's an illness among the emotions that needs to be cured if a person is going to be able to experience the fullness of spiritual healing. We have also seen how bad morals education and bad moral practice leads to this illness.

The individual must trust in the person who's trying to bring him the cure—not only to trust the person emotionally but intel-lectually as well. A flawless explanation of the morals of this case is necessary for true feeling to begin. Why? Because when the person begins to trust, this strong repressing emotion slowly begins to subside. As it slowly begins to subside, it allows the other emotion to come out, so that with our intelligence we can come to deal with it as would an adult.

Unfortunately, it often happens that this isn't the case. The person hasn't allowed this trust to happen when it should have been the normal progress that takes place in adolescence of dealing with all these things haltingly—whereby a person tries to discover what the truth of the thing is and either succeeds or fails, but is realistic about it. Instead, there's been no maturity in this regard at all, and this often is kept under wraps in a person with real difficulties for a long, long time.

In order for this process to be opened, the repressing emo-tion has to be withdrawn. That cannot occur without trust. So, the first thing the therapist or the person who is trying to bring about the cure must do is to form a relationship of trust with this individual. The patient must trust that the therapist is telling the truth and is interested in his or her good. This trust must include the truth.

Anger: 'Let It All Out'?

The passion of anger is an excellent example. Some people have difficulties with expressing anger and thus become doormats to other people. Pop psychologists would say, "Just get angry! Just get angry! Beat the wall! Just get angry!" It's irrational, because the anger isn't connected to anything true.

Not every emotional experience is a good one. If you have emotional difficulties, then simply having emotional experiences is not going to resolve them. It's like saying, "A person who's starving to death from malnutrition will have their physical difficulties resolved by just continually eating junk food." Many think that any kind of feeling is fine. It doesn't matter whether it is true or false, as long as it somehow expresses the feelings that are flawed. No, that's not true.

A person must understand, for example, how anger relates to the spiritual life. Is anger always evil? Should we always suppress it? Should we always destroy it? Well, what does Scripture say? As noted earlier, it says, "Be angry but do not sin" (Eph. 4:26). It doesn't say "never get angry." The Lord Himself, if you recall, was angry on at least one occasion when He drove the money changers from the temple, but He didn't lose his temper. I know there are preachers today who will say, "Jesus lost it. He just lost it in the temple." No, Jesus didn't lose it. He was exceedingly angry, but He did not lose His temper. There is a difference. Not just any emotional experience would do: it had to be one that corresponded to truth and to reason.

Dr. Baars gives an example of this. He said he went to the concentration camp with 100 people, and perhaps 98 of these died. He was one of the two that survived. He asked, "Why did I survive the experience in the concentration camp? Because my anger at the evil of my captors was so great that again, in the psychosomatic unity and body and spirit, it kept my adrenaline alive, my emotion of anger, so that I did not easily succumb to malnutrition or a disease. But it was an anger that I could never openly express—because if I openly expressed it, it would have meant my death." So, he was angry and did not sin. He did not let the sun go down on his anger.

The purpose of anger is to redress a wrong. If a person commits an equal wrong just to get his temper out because he simply wants to lose it, he usually says something unjust or in some context that's unjust—or, if it's really bad, he might even murder a person through anger, and then he's done even worse than the evil he was trying to address.

Instead, a person who realistically and virtuously deals with anger does not ignore wrongs done to him. He does not just become a doormat to everybody. Instead, he experiences anger but looks for the proper time and place to express it. Anger in itself is not evil. Anger is one of the eleven natural passions. True anger in man must be obedient to reason and to the truth. It is what we are angry about or how we express anger that can be evil. Our problem is that as a result of concupiscence, of possessiveness, and of the domineering inclination that comes to us from the Original Sin, it becomes easy for us to use anger as an excuse for any kind of conduct in which we seek to demonstrate our power over others.

The Value of Consequences

When a father, instead of giving his child a swat, canes his child and raises welts on the child's body, this is an example of the father trying to satisfy his egocentric emotions instead of just trying to connect a little physical punishment with the correction of the child. The object should be that child gets the idea of right and wrong. The idea is not that the child learns to save himself or herself practically from death over an infraction, but instead that he or she sees the truth about the misdeed. That's the real issue: getting the child's attention so he or she can see the truth of the case, and also to teach that there are consequences to our actions.

Today, many people do not want to have consequences at all. It is not uncommon to find children staying with their parents until they're twenty-five or thirty years of age and expecting their parents to pay for everything for them all the time. That doesn't allow them to become adults. Alcoholics Anonymous calls this kind of treatment "enabling." It masks as love for another but is actually an exaggerated self-love. We don't want others to think we are cruel, but we are cruel when we do not allow the other person the ability to become an adult, when we rob them of the ability to become an adult by constantly "saving" them from consequences when they don't really need to be saved anymore. At twenty-five or thirty years of age, they don't need to be saved anymore, and enabling this robs them of becoming responsible adults.

Neurosis of Abandonment

In addition to these types of emotional illness, Dr. Baars also discovered another type that is perhaps more prevalent in our society today. Oddly enough, Dr. Baars wrote a book called *Born Only Once* in which he compared Marilyn Monroe and Adolf Hitler to each other as two people who suffered from this modern difficulty, which is also created by our materialistic utilitarian culture. This is a different emotional problem because it is not caused by an emotional conflict but by an emotional underdevelopment. The whole contraceptive mentality has created in us a false idea: it tells us not that "it's good that you exist because you come from the hands of a loving Creator," but rather that "it's good that you exist because you're convenient to me."

Dr. Baars discovered that there were lots of people today who didn't have emotional conflicts in the way Freud would describe but rather were people who never experienced emotional growth. They could be captains of industry who run major corporations; they could be Army generals, Navy captains, or university professors but have an emotionally deprived family life. They couldn't experience being a parent at home. They couldn't experience the surrender that is necessary in order to nurture another human being because in their emotional life they were still three years old. This was due to the fact that their own parents did not affirm them as children.

Dr. Baars began to discover that there was a similarity between these people who are loved by their mothers and fathers not because they were good in themselves, but because they were useful or harmful to them, or convenient to them, and what he called a *neurosis of abandonment*. This neurosis is similar to what orphans feel. In other words, these individuals never had a loving parent who selflessly and disinterestedly loved them.

Of course, little children need this love to be emotionally expressed in the primary years. This is primarily the role of the mother. Teenagers need it to be intellectually expressed in the adolescent years. They need the intellectual affirmation of a father. Often lacking in family life today is the fact that the mothers communicate to the child that the child is not good simply because he exists, but because he is convenient to the mother. This may not be even consciously expressed in those words, but they may be communicated emotionally to the child through nonverbal signals. Fathers express this by being perpetual teenagers themselves, whereby they are never really present to their families. The spiritually absent father is a special problem in adolescence. The father might be repulsed by his son because his son is not at all the way he thought he should be, or perhaps the father smothers his son to make him like himself. In neither case does the child experience the disinterested love of a parent.

Many parents today want to be buddies to their children. That is not what a child needs—a buddy, a pal. What a child needs is someone who is self-surrendered enough and disinterested enough to be interested in the child's good for the child's own good—and that means disciplining him. Children who are raised in families with no real virtuous adults often end up being convinced that it is not good they exist. What should be experienced by merely being, they try to prove by doing. They need to prove to themselves that their existence is good because of what they accomplish.

Affirmation the Right Way

Marilyn Monroe had a terrible family life. She tried to prove to herself that it was good she existed and lovable in herself by becoming the sex goddess of the world. Hitler had a terrible family life, and he tried to prove that it was good he existed by conquering the world. Both lives ended in suicide because we cannot affirm ourselves. We must receive affirmation as a gift from the hands of a disinterested loving other.

God should be the primary giver of this gift, of course, but we do not see God; this emotional experience must come through someone who represents God, and the primary people who represent God in any person's life are the parents. The mother's emotional affirmation and the father's intellectual affirmation are equally necessary.

Dr. Baars said that affirmation is not a matter of doing things to people; it's a matter of an *attitude of being*—the fact that "I love you because you exist, not because of what you've done or haven't done, not because you are winner or a loser." Affirmation is not just being nice to people, but it's a matter of tough love, as an attitude to being. One communicates to another that it is good that they exist because they come from the power of a loving creator and not because they are useful. Glances, tones of voice and on a higher level personal interest can express: "it is good that you exist objectively" and not "it is good that you exist because you are useful to me." To the question: Why did God make me?, the *Baltimore Catechism* replies: "God make me to show forth his goodness and to make me happy with him in heaven." This may involve being harsh if one knows the other will not be crushed and it is for their good

Freed for the Truth

In one of Dr. Barr's talks, he recalls how the apostle Peter confessed Jesus to be the Son of God, but then, after Jesus predicted His Passion, Peter told Jesus that He shouldn't suffer. Jesus then looked at Peter and said, "Get behind me, Satan, you're trying to make me trip and fall" (Matt. 16:23). Jesus was affirming Peter because He was telling Peter the truth. Imagine you were in a public gathering, and Christ walked up to you and said, "Get behind Me, Satan, you're trying to make Me trip and fall." That wouldn't be nice. However, Peter was being honed to become the head of the Church, and Jesus knew that he could take it; He wanted Peter to experience a deeper clarity. He was telling him the truth, and in this way He was intellectually affirming him.

There are many people today who experience an emotional illness in which, in all relationships, they look for the mother or the father they never had. Oftentimes marriages end in divorce because instead of regarding his wife as an equal, a man marries a woman so he can find his mother figure and wants to be treated like a little boy. Sometimes a woman marries a man because she wants him to be a father figure to her, and she wants to be treated like a little girl. Neither one of them can experience the adult surrender that is necessary for the healing of the spirit on which the true marital relationship is based. We experience this in the clergy, too: many times the ecclesiastical superiors don't affirm their priests because they do not tell them the truth, and often they do not even confront them personally when there is a problem to be addressed.

In healing of the spirit, it is the truth that is the issue. We are not being freed *from* the truth, but we're being freed *for* the truth. This alone can be the source of true healing of the psychological difficulty in the Spirit. An affirming adult is taking the place of God is aiding the person to discover the truth about themselves.

6

Psychic Healing and Grace

Mortification Therapy

Dr. Baars pioneered a new approach to therapy for obsessive-compulsive neurotics called *mortification therapy*. This therapy has sometimes been very controversial with confessors and moral theologians. It would therefore seem useful to devote a whole chapter to it. First, it needs to be stated that spiritual authors like Fr. Jordan Aumann found the ideas in the books of Dr. Baars to be in fundamental agreement with Catholic doctrine. As his ideas bear a superficial resemblance to moral permissiveness, clarification is in order.

The problem is especially urgent as today's climate is loaded with self-help techniques that are permissive and misleading. Some people think that in order to cure problems with sexual integration or assertion, all one needs to do is to be ordered to experience these things even if the actions are sinful. Some moral theologians after Vatican II proposed new moral norms that basically permitted almost any actions. Dr. Baars is very clear that true healing cannot occur for this problem until both moral theologians and psychiatrists cooperate in the process of guidance based on authentic Catholic moral teaching.

The obsessive-compulsive neurotic is fundamentally very intelligent and naturally capable of full integration but suffers from bad moral education and the fact that his or her passions have been formed based on this education. "These mistaken interpretations are most likely to be formed when educators—parents, teachers, relatives, religious instructors—convey to the young person, directly or indirectly, that sex is actually potentially harmful, if not an occasion of sin." This mistaken impression can be given in a variety of ways. It can be the result of positive teaching or of the omission of that teaching, or even of the manner in which sexual matters or other matters such as anger are discussed.

Strategies for healing

Two strategies form the cornerstone for healing of this condition. The first is to explain the inherent goodness of the feelings themselves involved. This does not mean moral goodness, but natural goodness. The *Catechism of the Catholic Church* explains this well: "In themselves passions are neither good nor evil. They are morally qualified to the extent that they effectively engage reason and will" (n. 1767). The feelings of pleasure or even the passion of love is a natural response to perceived good. Dr. Baars gives the example of a rose: "[...] if I love a rose it is not because *I* arouse this emotion or will it, but because the qualities of the rose—shape, color, fragrance—stimulate my feeling of liking." In the case of sexuality, though one might be able to write a treatise on the goods involved in the conjugal act, this does not arrive at the feelings. Pope St. John Paul II's teachings on "the theology of the body" have done much to encourage this proper understanding.

Dr. Baars continues: "to enable the patient to develop this *feeling knowledge* the therapist must also help him to rid himself of the cause of this repressing fear or energy, i.e., his usefulness judgment that sex is harmful." This involves giving the patient that advice that he should change his judgment from I *must not* experience pleasure in sexual matters to I *may* experience pleasure in these matters, or from I *must not* feel anger to I *may* feel anger. The point must be stressed that such advice is not given to people who are well-formed concerning these feelings. This is only given to obsessive-compulsive neurotics. The reason is that the neurotic will tell you he can control his behavior and feelings in this regard, but he does not do so from a choice creating a virtue. He only does this by using one emotion to control another.

This is the essence of mortification therapy. This seems strange because Catholics have been used to applying the term "mortification" to suppressing feelings like pleasure at sexuality and anger because they can lure us into sin. If mortification is sometimes indicated for pleasures that lead to sin, it is also indicated for these passions like fear and energy which are out of control in the neurotic.

The usual difficulty for moralists and confessors is that when these repressed feelings begin to emerge, they may often lead to morally evil acts such as self-abuse or masturbation. The psychiatrist is not to recommend these acts since he is the voice of reason in the patient's life. To do so would constitute reason recommending something intrinsically evil, which is impossible. The same would be true for anger.

A temporary toleration

Nevertheless, since the patient cannot control these acts except by a repressive means, the psychiatrist and confessor may have to tolerate these acts for a time while the repressed feelings are emerging from being buried alive. It goes without saying that it would be against justice to involve another in these acts. Normally, obsessive compulsive neurotics have a strong sense of justice, so if this is explained to them, they understand.

Dr. Baars maintains that *only* for the time when these feelings are emerging, the therapist must say: 1) you may do everything and 2) for you, there are no rules. Objectively, of course, there *are* rules, but the person interprets the whole idea of rule in a wrong sense. They must be allowed to recover the correct sense. This takes time and patience, and the presumption morally would be that the person has no moral determination over these particular actions while reintegration is happening.

Two magisterial sources may be helpful here to quiet the fear of the confessor. First, the *Catechism of the Catholic Church*. "To form an equitable judgment about the subject's moral responsibility and to guide pastoral action, one must take into account the affective immaturity, force of acquired habit, conditions of anxiety, or other psychological or social factors that can lessen, if not even reduce to a minimum, moral culpability" (n. 2352). Pope Pius XII taught a similar doctrine: "From this a conclusion follows for psychotherapy. In the presence of material sin it cannot remain neutral. It can, for the moment, tolerate what remains inevitable. But it must know that God cannot justify such an action. With still less reason can psychotherapy counsel a patient to commit material sin on the ground that it will be without subjective guilt. Such a counsel would be erroneous if this action were regarded as necessary for psychic easing of the patient and thus as being part of the treatment. One may never counsel a conscious action which would be a deformation and not an image of divine perfection."

The obvious point here is that no one can recommend someone do an evil action. On the other hand, they can allow the patient to experience feelings in regard to the thing repressed, which may lead to some action that constitutes a material sin. Since they cannot control this action except by further repression through the emotional illness, the therapist may tolerate this action as concomitant to the emerging emotion. Toleration here means one does not command it or forbid it. The therapist does this with the proper explanation given of all the moral aspects involved. One might say that, for most people, this is an evil. But in the case of the patient, it is perhaps only a venial sin, and the alternative is to encourage the emotional problem they have.

Passivity is much more important than activity when one is dealing with this type of neurotic. The therapist must live the same doctrine he is teaching. Dr. Baars is clear: "There cannot be any fundamental conflict between sound moral theology and sound philosophical anthropology."

Opening up to joy

The last directive that is a part of this therapy is this: "The plea-sure you experience as a result of abiding by the other directives is the most perfect thing for you." The patient has never related to those goods that he has repressed in an authentic way with real joy. Once the positive experience of these goods emerges and he is able to address them in a mature way, then things begin to fall into place properly. The joy of the person becomes other-centered rather than self-centered because he can experience the goods as they were meant to be. The essence of the correct guidance for the normal and the wounded person is to be present like God. This is what parents must do and also what God does.

Dr. Baars summarizes this therapy: "*The essence of a healthy upbringing* is an attitude which is in fundamental agreement with that of God. This means that they [educators] respect the child's need to become a free human being and abstain from anything that will interfere with that freedom, such as undue stimulation of potentially repressing emotions. This they can do only if they have a reasonable trust in the basic goodness of every human being, i.e., that man has continued to be oriented toward the good in spite of the imperfection of his nature caused by Original Sin. This trust implies that the educator believes that the child will learn also from his faults and mistakes, because they interfere with his finding what he really wants; that which is truly good and fulfilling of his nature."

The Nature of Grace

Because we have intelligence, it is necessary for us to be able to arrive at Heaven in order for us to experience human integrity. Grace is the means by which we do that. Adam and Eve were created in this grace, but they lost it in the Original Sin. Christ recovers grace for us. But Adam and Eve also had some very important gifts that expressed the integrity of their hearts toward this grace, and we do not get those back.

Grace not only elevates us to prepare for Heaven—which it did for Adam and Eve before the sin—but also, since we've fallen below our nature, it's necessary for us to experience sanctifying grace so that we can experience the healing of our spirits. The healing of our spirits, therefore, is caused primarily by the Holy Spirit as the supernatural good is sent into our souls in baptism. In Baptism, we also receive what's called a character—a conformity to Christ as priest, prophet, and king—that we never lose.

But we *can* lose sanctifying grace. This is the principle of our healing. Since God gave us this grace so that we might experience intimacy with Him, it's necessary for us not only to experience healing of our sins through grace but also to progressively experience being elevated in our minds, in our wills, in our consciousness as people, to experience intimacy with the Holy Trinity. We—and that's every Christian, not just monks and nuns in monasteries—are called to the fullness of union with God on earth, which is called contemplation. Why don't many of us experience this contemplation in its fullness? The real reason is either because we do not seek it or because we have faulty understandings of God and His love through a bad anthropology that can result either from emotional problems or bad teaching or both.

Contemplation: Our Interior Castle

The Scriptures tell us that grace is like a seed sown in the fields of our souls. Care is necessary for this seed to grace. Saint Teresa of Avila likens this growth of the seed to entering a castle, the interior castle, in which there are seven mansions. Why a castle? Because it's a large building. Why mansions? Because these are large dwelling places. Christ tells us in the Gospel that when we receive grace, the Holy Trinity will come to dwell in our hearts. We must have a fit dwelling place in order to receive this Holy Spirit. This is what growth in prayer is: to allow this grace, which is a very change in our souls, to influence what we think and how we love.

Saint Teresa defined prayer as a loving conversation among friends. Well, who is our friend in this case? The Blessed Trinity—the Father, the Son, and the Holy Spirit. If we want to grow in prayer, if we want to grow in divine intimacy, then we must be open to receiving this grace. We must be prepared. The difficulty is that there are many people who have a lot of mistaken ideas about what growth in prayer in a deep sense involves. How do we enter into the interior castle and begin to heal our wills?

Prayer as Loving Conversation

In previous chapters we discussed healing our emotions, which sometimes involve natural means like therapy. Healing our wills involves always a moral means, and this moral means is grace.

Some people have the idea that in order for them to enter deeply into a communion with God, they must find the right method. Americans are great at this, because we are very practical people. We don't like to be confused by long explanations. We want, in a way, a "fast-food religion": "Just tell me the steps I have to go through, and I'll go through them; I'll be efficient about it, and I should be able to experience communion with God just like that, if I could only find the right method."

There are some very great and highly recommended methods of prayer. However, St. Teresa of Avila did not talk about methods, because prayer is not basically an efficient experience. Many people want to become instant mystics. There is no such thing.

Prayer is a loving conversation among friends, and contemplation involves a communion of hearts. The classic imagery of this has always been a marriage. If you think you can find an efficient method to instantaneously produce contemplation, you may as well suggest that you can find the efficient method for instantaneously producing the ideal marriage.

Some people today adopt Eastern meditation techniques. They sit with their legs crossed on the floor, do their mantras and breathing exercises, and think that when they produce sort of an alternate state of consciousness that they are entering into communion with the living God. They think they can turn it on and off by their own power. You may as well suggest that you can have the ideal marriage by sitting with your legs crossed in a lotus position, doing some breathing exercises and producing an alternate state of consciousness, but without ever thinking about your wife or husband, or cooking any meals, or working, or communicating with your spouse. This isn't realistic with someone we can see. How can it possibly be realistic with someone we can't see?

The Cross Calls us to Lose Our Egos

Although methods of meditation are helpful for focusing our attention on Christ, union with Christ and union with God is not something we can efficiently produce in an instantaneous way. People who want an easy prayer also think they can develop an easy virtue. They want a religion with no trouble. They want a religion that does not involve crucifixion. Of course, the biggest crucifixion we face is trying to lose our egos in order to serve others in everyday life.

When we are baptized, we get back God's grace, but we don't get back the gifts Adam and Eve had. We now experience concupiscence; we now experience moral and emotional weakness. Dealing with that moral and emotional weakness is the greatest suffering we can possibly have; in fact, the pain we experience in seeking to allow God to free us from our unbridled egotism is our participation in the Cross of Christ. Saint Paul tells us that we make up what's lacking in the sufferings of Christ (cf. Col. 1:24). What could possibly be lacking in the sufferings of Christ? Nothing, as far as their ability to redeem us and the whole world. What is lacking is their application to my life. That application demands, first of all, that if I am going to be prepared and open to His grace, I must address the results of this unbridled ego in both a positive and negative sense.

In the analogy of growth of the seed of the kingdom, we must first address our faults and sins. This is analogous to the way we prepare soil, which is to rip it open by plowing it. The soil must also be weeded. If the soil being prepared to receive the seed had feelings, then when one plows it open and pulls out the weeds, the soil experiences pain. The same is true for us in preparing ourselves for the action of grace. The positive aspect is the assiduous desire to practice the virtues of each person's state in life.

The Problem With Seeking the Extraordinary

Preparation for entering the interior castle involves opening our-selves and preparing ourselves to receive God's way of doing things, God's way of looking at things. Some people have the idea that the best way to prepare themselves for this is to "have some spectacular experience." Religion does involve spectacular experiences, such as miracles or visions. "If only I could have a little vision. If only I could maybe suffer the stigmata. If only I could have some unusual, extraordinary gift and be able to heal people, something like that." Some people who were involved in the Charismatic Renewal used to be upset because they couldn't speak in tongues, because it was so unusual. "If only I could have that, then I could be sure that I'm growing in prayer."

Many people try to stimulate their religious ideas by constantly feeding themselves with the experiences of visionaries. One spiri-tual author, Fr. Thomas Dubay, S.M., says in one of his books that most people wouldn't walk across the street to experience a hid-den act of patience in a family, but they'll sell all they possess and cross oceans to sites of visions and miracles. They will not stop at one, but will try to keep feeding themselves on these experiences. Yet every spiritual author tells us that one hidden act of patience is worth more for growth in prayer than all the visions, miracles, and spectacular experiences combined.

Why does God send extraordinary experiences? Why are there visionaries? What was the message at Lourdes? "Pray the rosary, pray for sinners." All these things exist to stimulate people to do hidden acts of patience. They are the means, not the end. They are an attempt to get us to see how important God is in our life, especially for those of us who become lukewarm.

The third great difficulty many people have in trying to experience growth in prayer is the fact that they would like to be in another situation than the one they are in presently. "I could become a moral religious person. I could grow in prayer. I could really experience the presence of God ... if I didn't have to live with you. You're the reason I can't become a holy person. If only I didn't have this family. If only I didn't have this job. If only I didn't have this illness. If only I didn't have this boss." You could go down the list. "If only, if only, if only, I were in another situation, then I could truly become a religious person."

Experiencing God In Suffering

If it's true that our growth in prayer has to do with experiencing the interior communion that we have in Christ, then obviously it doesn't depend on our external situation. The external setting is of comparative indifference. In fact, many people have become very holy by suffering in the midst of a trying situation.

One of the things that has always fascinated me about the Catholic psychologist Dr. Conrad Baars is the fact that he grew up in Holland during World War II. He was a medical student who joined the underground and helped Allied fliers to escape. The Nazis caught him and put him in the concentration camp at Buchenwald, an experience he survived for two or three years. Here's what he said of his experience in the concentration camp, certainly a place where it's very hard, by external setting, to be aware of the presence of God: "One of the French priests imprisoned in the concentration camp of Buchenwald once said, 'When one speaks of the privileged to come out alive from Buchenwald, one all should consider the fact that it's been a greater privilege to have been sent there.'"[7]

[7] Conrad Baars, *Doctor*, 186.

A privilege to be sent to a concentration camp? How could someone say something so silly? "And even this without the first is a privilege indeed," he continued. Without surviving it was a privilege? Doesn't this sound stupid to you? He continues:

> Yes, it has been a privilege, even though in the beginning I rebelled against God's holy Will. And in my conceit, the man answers as to why it had to me and not my neighbor who had to undergo such misery. But as time passed, my eyes were opened and I began to see what before I could not comprehend. I had come to understand the real value of the things I once thought important and worth living for. When life was sweet and carefree, I had valued money, for example, because I thought it could buy me happiness. It could not, however, buy my freedom. The best of foods and wines and all the delicacies to please the tongue and once seemed important, yet bread and wine suffice to keep body and soul together. I valued a carefree life, reaping the fruits of my education. However, the miseries of prison life taught me the real meaning of life. I had not valued God and His commands. And now in prison, I realize that I could not live without Him. That life without God has no meaning. Buchenwald was a hard and bitter experience but it was an advantage to those who knew how to profit from it. Why does God permit wars and concentration camps? Again, the answer is simple, because He loves us because He wants to bring back to His fold, those who otherwise in a life of pleasures and lusts would've been lost.[8]

[8] Baars, *Heart*, 186.

Addressing Lust

This is why the real issue for healing of the spirit, then, is not in finding the right situation, but in addressing your lust. What is lust?

When we think of lust, we think of sexual pleasure. Lust, however, is a lot more than that. I already explained this a bit. Let me make it clear again. Lust is signified by the three "gray areas" of life: my ability to obey another (in sexual pleasure, it's true), the pleasures of food and drink, and the power that money can bring. Lust has to do with the desire to dominate another human being. These "gray areas" are like the weeds that choke off the seed. In order for us to remedy, cure, or heal this desire to dominate, we need to allow the action of the Holy Spirit to influence our positive actions. What can we do for another in our lives as Christ would act?

To enter the castle, the first thing we must address is not trying to find the right situation, the right method, some extraordinary phenomenon, or some mystical visions. The way we enter the castle is in our ordinary lives as husbands, wives, children, employees, or members in religious or community life. We must realize that we must root out our faults, address our lusts, and seek positive occasions in which we are able to actually give ourselves to another person according to the ordinary duties of our state. This is the place where we actually fertilize the soil, where we water it, where we pull out the weeds, where the plow goes through it and rips it open.

7

The Three Ages of the Spiritual Life

Stages to Healing of Our Spirits

As we saw in the previous chapter, to enter the interior castle does not involve particular prayer methods, spectacular experiences, or finding exactly the right situation. Instead it occurs in the ordinary duties of our life and has two basic prongs to it. One of these prongs is negative—the routing out of faults, addressing our lusts—and the other prong is positive, the desire to grow in the virtues so as to lead a virtuous life. As in the parable of the seed and the sower, we must open our wills or prepare our soil in order to receive the action or life of the seed.

Every single Christian is called to the perfection of what grace offers to them. This perfection of grace is not just for consecrated men and women in monasteries, although they are called to this perfection in a special way by "living the contemplative life." Yet every single human being is called to live contemplation according to the duties of their state. Saint Francis de Sales used to call this "living the devout life."

According to Saint Teresa of Avila and many spiritual authors, there are three basic stages to the progressive healing of our spirits, so as to enter into communion with God in order to live this contemplative life. The first is called *spiritual infancy*, also known by a fancy two-bit term, the *purgative way*. It is called "purgative" because addressing our lusts and seeking to grow in virtue when we don't have an easy virtue now is very difficult.

This first stage in our conversion experience involves the pain of rooting out faults and growing in the virtues. It is characterized by detachment. It causes suffering; it is our share in the cross of Christ. Yet it is the necessary place where we do our part to take the weeds out of the soil, to plow the ground, to fertilize it, and to water it in order to open it to bearing the life force that is present in the seed of grace given to us in the sacraments, especially in the Sacrament of Baptism.

The second great way to this life is a little more mature than the purgative way, which is a type of spiritual adolescence. This second way, which we will deal with later in this book, is the *illuminative way*.

Finally, our spiritual progress is completed in this world when we truly know as God knows and love as God loves, when we truly adopt God's attitude toward ourselves and toward our world, which is the way we were created to be in the beginning. This is normal psychology; this is what man should normally be, an in-graced being. This third way is called *spiritual maturity*, also known as the *unitive way*. It also is called by the analogous word suggestive of Scripture, *spousal union with God*. Every one of us is called to this union, for every one of us is called to a marriage with God or Christ.

Learning Self-Restraining Love

With the purgative way, we enter into spiritual infancy. As we've noted here, there are two basic parts to living this way in our ordinary lives as we seek to live the Gospel and the will of Christ.

The first part involves rooting out our faults or lusts. Recall that according to Scripture, in the letters of St. John, there are three basic forms of lust: the lust of the flesh, the lust of the eyes, and the pride of life. The lust of the flesh pertains to the pleasures associated with sexuality, food, and drink. These pleasurers often lead us to the keystone of lust, which is the desire to dominate our situation or another person rather than surrender to God. The lust of the eyes has to do with always looking elsewhere, always being jealous, envious, or possessive — always wanting something that another person has. That can be health, beauty, strength, money, job, anything. We are always looking because we think it can bring us power, which we see as the solution to our lives.

Then, of course, pride of life has to do with our desire not to surrender ourselves to anyone or to any situation but rather to have everyone surrender to us. This is characteristic of the action of the devil. The devil is an ego that wants to absorb all other egos, to feed on them. And when we participate in this special form of lust — which is found in the sin of pride, the deepest of all sins — we want to absorb the egos of others. We do not want to give; all we want to do is take. We have the grasping hand.

This is just the opposite of what St. Paul says of Christ in his letter to the Philippians: "though he was in the form of God, did not count equality with God a thing to be grasped, but emptied himself, taking the form of a servant" (Phil. 2:6-7). Who grasped at being like God? We're all supposed to be like God because of grace, but who grasped at it? Adam and Eve grasped at it in the Original Sin.

Detachment

The purgative way begins with addressing the fact that we have moral weakness about ourselves. Make no mistake about it, there is no one who does not have faults they need to root out. There's only one person in the history of the human race who had no faults: the Blessed Virgin Mary. Every single one of us must address this difficulty in our lives. The act of addressing this difficulty is called *detachment*. If something is attached to us because we have a disordered love based on our disordered ego, a love of something in this world, then we cannot open ourselves and surrender ourselves to God.

There are many mistaken ideas of detachment. Many people believe—and this comes from the ancient philosophy called Stoicism—that in order to be a virtuous person, in order to experience detachment, generosity, and the loss of the ego, that we must completely deny all of our feelings, all of our emotions. We must pretend that they do not exist. Because our desires for pleasure and to avoid pains can often lead us to sin, we must absolutely root them out completely—not only these desires, but these feelings. We become unfeeling, like a stick or a stone.

A good image of this some of you may have seen in the famous 1943 movie, *The Song of Bernadette*. Bernadette's first mother superior practices this form of Stoicism; she's basically a dried-up prune. She says to Bernadette in a deadpan expression, "All throughout sacred time, God has only come to those who have suffered. How can you say you have seen the Blessed Virgin, when you haven't ever suffered as I have? Look at my eyes. They burn like the very fires of hell from lack of sleep that I will not give them. My lips are parched from constant prayer. My hands are wracked from serving God. My back is now from cold stone floors."

This is presented as a kind of spiritual perfection. It's not! The rooting out of faults does not involve the destruction of the passions, putting them to death, even though we often use terms like "mortification" to refer to denying certain passion experiences that might lead us to sin. Why not? God made the passions. They're a part of our psyche. We cannot destroy them completely and remain human. God made the pleasures. These things are good in and of themselves. Why do they become occasions of lust or weakness to us? Because of our lack of surrender to God in grace.

The Modern Problem of Affirmation Neurosis

As we have seen, in addition to the traditional obsessive-compulsive neurosis, Drs. Baars and Terruwe pioneered a new discovery concerning emotional illness. Dr. Baars recounts that he had been practicing psychotherapy for several months in that traditional way on a patient. This patient showed no sign of progress. One day the patient remarked, "'Doctor, nothing you say has any effect on me. For six months I have been sitting here hoping you would take me to your heart ... you have been blind to my needs.' These words came as a revelation to us. Evidently this patient, whose mother has been an extremely cold and businesslike woman, felt like a child. She needed only one thing—namely to be treated in a tender, motherly fashion."

In examining the type of emotional distress this patient suffered from, Dr. Baars discovered that she had emotional characteristics very similar to those traditionally exhibited by abandoned children. Though she had a mother and father, and so was not objectively abandoned, she had never been disinterestedly loved by them or shown any affection by them when she was a child. He came to understand that these characteristics did not fit into the traditional definition of neurosis as an emotional conflict because there was no conflict between the passions such as occurs in repression. He called this new emotional difficulty *deprivation neurosis* because it is due to a lack of development of the feelings rather than a conflict in them.

There are a number of important differences between repression and deprivation. "The chief characteristics of deprivation neurosis [are]: (1) the insufficiently developed emotional life, with the consequent inability to direct oneself in a normal fashion with others; (2) a feeling of uncertainty which manifests itself usually in fear; and (3) feelings of inferiority and inadequacy, with or without feelings of guilt, which lead either to depression or to aggressive behavior. On the other hand, as distinct from repressive neuroses, we see the absence of excessive fear or energy; an open uninhibited attitude toward sense goods; and a static clinical symtomatology."

A Common Malady

Dr. Baars believes this neurosis is by far the more common in today's Western utilitarian culture rooted in the "me first" mentality. In his book, *Born Only Once*, he enumerates the following characteristics of this syndrome: (1) the inability to relate to other to form intimate friendships or a truly loving marital relationship; (2) feelings of uncertainty and insecurity; (3) feelings of inferiority and inadequacy; and (4) increasing feelings of depression.

Dr. Baars called the therapy for this problem *affirmation* and later regretted his choice of this word. Many people look upon affirmation as *doing* something for others. Dr. Baars calls this *pseudo-affirmation*. One glaring example of this he gives is not telling others the truth because one is afraid to hurt their feelings. Truth is very important to treating the unaffirmed person. The unaffirmed person "pushes the 'button of affirmation' in counseling; who devises new affirmation techniques for group encounters; who stresses emotions and feelings at the expense of moral truths; who make a living turning out self-help books and offering pop-psychology courses which do not consider, or are ignorant of, the intellectual and spiritual needs of man. [...] But it is precisely because they *do* (and not because they *are*) that their services and help to unaffirmed people must be labeled pseudo-affirming."

Affirmation is largely about presence, both emotional and intellectual presence. Everyone has had the experience of talking to someone who was physically present to them but distracted by something else and was not listening. This is somewhat like the experience of the deprivation neurotic. They grew up in a family but never received the gift of themselves emotionally from the hands of a loving other who loved them with disinterested love. Instead, they were encouraged to substitute either their intellect or something at an early age to prove that they were lovable. This, of course, is not like the love of God for us, who loves us into existence prior to anything we have done or accomplished. Human beings, especially parents stand in the place of God. and so by their affection for their children they give the children the gift of themselves each according to their age and even sex. Boys and girls receive affirmation in different ways, and the influence of both parents in necessary. There is not a natural foundation in these people for the surrender required in detachment.

The Role Of Sympathy

Emotional affirmation of the therapist, who must be present to them, is very important here for healing. "They must come to *feel* that they are not alone, and that there is someone to whom they can entrust themselves with whom they are really safe." The person suffering from this may be able to write an academic treatise on the goodness of being, but they are unable to apply this to their own feelings. The sympathy of the therapist is therefore important for healing here, always preserving the proper distance from the patient. One must always keep in mind that this difficulty is caused by an emotional underdevelopment in which the sufferer spends their whole lives searching for someone to serve as a surrogate mother or father.

Emotional affirmation is not enough. Though approval is very important to people lacking affirmation, it is not a matter of being "nice." This is still pseudo-affirmation because it avoids the issue. "These affirmation techniques usually are practiced in an atmosphere of permissiveness and 'sensitivity' directed at not 'hurting anyone's feelings'."

Intellectual affirmation is necessary especially for teenagers and especially for the father. The spiritual presence of the father in the home is absolutely necessary. This is especially true for boys and often is painfully lacking in their regard. The father must not only be an emotional support, but he also must provide intelligent direction, which includes punishment and telling the truth, even if people get their feelings hurt. Fathers who may be physically but not spiritually present in the home cannot fill this void. "No wonder that the lack of affirmation by the father caused greater psychological trauma in boys than in girls."

Christ practiced this sort of authentic affirmation by telling the truth. As I explained already, Dr. Baars says that in the celebrated incident from the life of Christ in which Peter forbid him to suffer and Christ called him Satan in public, Christ was affirming Peter. He knew Peter was capable of receiving this correction, and he had a great role in mind for him as head of the Church. Peter had grown strong enough to receive such correction. This demonstrates well that "no authentic teaching is possible by a pseudo-affirmer, much less by a self-affirmer" (someone who tries to prove to themselves they are lovable by something they have done). "The pseudo-affirming atmosphere of being 'nice,' and saying the right things, of being tolerant and permissive, reveals the lack of authenticity of the person claiming to 'practice affirmation'."

Dr. Baars thinks that this neurosis is more prominent today because of families broken by divorce, birth control, abortion (the greatest lack of affirmation), and the general utilitarian attitude toward people common in our materialistic culture. If this is true, then it is important that communities, seminaries, and even persons considering marriage be aware that their possible candidates may be suffering from this emotional difficulty. Today's youth are very good people, but sometimes they lack any real moral fiber for dealing with difficult people or correction. They sometimes enter communities or marriage seeking to find the mother and father they never had. They cannot live up to all that these vocations demand until this problem is dealt with.

This is not a judgment of the moral worth of the individual. No amount of good will can fix an emotional difficulty any more than good will can fix a broken arm. Prospective community members who may suffer from this should be encouraged to seek to resolve the situation before entering. Any sort of progress in the spiritual life must admit the possible contribution of this emotional difficulty to the initial experience of detachment required.

This is important because environment has a heavy influence over the cure of someone like this. Most communities and parishes simply cannot tolerate someone who is unable to behave emotionally like an adult. They are so busy doing their things and carrying on their lives that they have no real time for someone who looks like an adult but demands the care, attention, and understanding of a child.

Religious communities make demands on members with little security in the environment and a great number of different personality types. A person with this emotional problem should not be allowed to enter until he or she has some resolution of this problem. The community may make the problem worse despite having the best intentions in the world. If the person is in community, a positive and secure environment is necessary for him or her to experience any healing. Normally this cannot be easily done if the person is treated as an adult member. The person is emotionally five years old even though he or she otherwise may be an intelligent and competent person at work.

Why We Experience Weakness

Detachment, then, is not a question of destroying the passions. Of course, we have to deny our feelings in certain cases if they're going to lead us to sin. But why do we have a weakness about our passions or our feelings? We have a weakness about our passions because of our weakness of our will. Sin is primarily in the will. The question we have to address is our will, the desires of our will, the loves of our will, and how we put our love for our own good ahead of the love of the good for others.

We must have an authentic kind of self-love. There's a good kind of self-love, but this kind of self-love is part of a bigger picture. Remember that we find ourselves by losing ourselves. We can only experience fullness by a sincere gift of ourselves to another. This means that instead of grasping or taking the other self, the only way that we can truly be like Christ—the only way we can truly experience spiritual healing—is to give ourselves to another. And when we're not doing that—or when we're unable to do that, or when we refuse to do that—that's when we know we need to be detached.

Proper Use of Goods

What are some signs that one needs to be detached? One sign is when we use any good thing that God has given us in a manner in which God did not intend it. For example, why did God will marriage? For three reasons—fidelity, friendship, and family. First, fidelity shows indissolubility. The persons of the Trinity don't leave each other; the Father, Son, and Holy Spirit never get divorced. Nor does Christ divorce the Church by coming down from the Cross; He shows the enduring and eternal character of this relationship.

Secondly, God willed marriage so we would experience a union of friendship. That's a little bit more than the feeling of being in love, which is a storm of emotions that often passes. Love often precedes marriage, but the honeymoon experience doesn't endure for your whole life. What does endure are the various goods that a husband and wife have in common.

Thirdly, the marital relationship exists in order to bring forth little people to grow in the love of God and to populate Heaven. When a person looks upon his or her marriage as an attempt to use, to dominate, or to manipulate the ego of the other, he or she is saying, "You're good not because you exist, but you're good because you make me feel good." When these relationships are perverted by the practice of contraception, by the practice of living together, by all the different difficulties that occur in sexual relationships, then we know they are being used in a manner for which God did not intend them.

Of course, we do not want to admit that. We want to think it's always something wrong with the other person. Jesus talks about the plank in our own eye and the splinter in the other person's eye. We never want to admit there's something wrong with us. A person who lacks affirmation simply finds this beyond this true self-knowledge.

The positive aspect of detachment is growth in virtue. Saint Thomas Aquinas says that the way to root out faults cannot consist merely in gritting our teeth and saying, "I won't commit any faults." What we must do is to positively practice those virtues that are contrary to our faults. When we do that, we form our character in a positive way so that our faults have less influence on us. It's like watering the soil, not just pulling out the weeds.

Humility and the Duties of State

The deepest of these vices is pride. The contrary virtue to the vice of pride is humility. A person, therefore, who wants to lose his or her ego must find and accept occasions to practice humility.

What is humility? Many people have the idea that humility is self-deprecation — strong men telling themselves they're weak, beautiful women telling themselves they're ugly, intelligent people telling themselves they're stupid. What is humility? I saw a great definition: "Humility does not mean thinking less of yourself. It's not self-deprecation. Humility means thinking of yourself less."

What do the duties that my state in life demand of me? To give of myself to another — not because I get something back, but because I realize all the wonderful things I have that I can offer to their service. This can only be the result of someone able to practice self-restraining love. What's the difference between machismo and masculinity? A machismo person is a person who uses all the masculine strength, anger, and support to take from others for their own selves; they serve themselves. Whereas a man is masculine who, as a person, uses all those things to serve others, to give himself to others, to support them. For a married man, that means especially to serve and support his wife and his children. He doesn't look at his wife as his servant, but rather looks at himself as the servant to his wife.

Grace, of course, instills this habit, but by nature a person also would experience more joy in serving others if he were healed emotionally. The virtues do not act in a vacuum. Although a person may be virtuous despite the disorder in the character caused by either emotional conflict or immaturity, a virtuous person is more at peace because his or her character is naturally disposed to order. Saint Francis de Sales once said:

> Opportunities for the great virtues like the practice of fortitude, magnanimity and magnificence do not often occur but gentleness, moderation, integrity and humility—gentleness, moderation, integrity and humility are virtues for which all the actions of our lives should be colored. There are virtues nobler than these but the practice of these is more necessary. Among the virtues, we should prefer that which suits our duty best and not that which is most to our taste. And although everyone ought to have all the virtues, yet not everyone is bound to practice them to the same extent. Each ought to give himself especially to those that are required by the kind of life to which he is called.

The Beginning of Growth: An Influx of Light and Love

Progressive healing of the spirit begins with spiritual infancy, in the purgative way, where we begin to seek growth in grace and in prayer. In this way, we first take seriously our conversion to Gospel living, and we do so within the ordinary duties of our state, not by seeking something spectacular or out of the ordinary. As fathers, mothers, husbands, wives, children, employees, consecrated religious, priests, or single persons, we embrace our duties of state according to what Christ has asked us to do in the Gospels.

This is done first by addressing those areas of our lives where we have weakness. Secondly, and perhaps more powerfully, we seek to remedy our weaknesses by emphasizing our strengths. In other words, we practice the contrary virtue to whatever our sins or lusts may be. With any excess or defect, we practice the contrary virtue, and this helps us to resolve the spiritual weaknesses within us.

An interesting thing happens when a person becomes accustomed to addressing his or her weaknesses and begins to practice growth in the contrary virtues. When we open ourselves more and prepare ourselves by an act of our wills to receive the grace God has given us, God takes us at our word and begins to give us an influx of His infinite light and love to experience. Through this influx, God is trying to elevate us from our merely human way of looking at things to a divine way of looking at things, which is the perspective of faith. Remember, grace, the divine indwelling of the Trinity, is given to us in order to change our way of looking at ourselves in the world, to prepare ourselves for Heaven. This is so that we on earth can adopt God's perspective in order that we might know as God knows, and love as God loves. This is not a human way of looking at things, but God's way.

When, therefore, God finds a soul prepared to receive Him, He takes that soul at his word, and the seed begins to grow and blossom. The life begins to flow in us—we as the branches, He as the vine—and we begin to adopt what St. Paul says before he cites the famous hymn in Philippians that reads, "though he was in the form of God, did not count equality with God a thing to be grasped" (Phil. 2:5). Paul introduces that hymn by stating, "Your attitude must be that of Christ" (see Phil 2:5). In other words, we no longer stand at the cross looking up, but we begin to adopt Christ's attitude from the cross, looking down. This morphs into the second great way of prayer: spiritual adolescence or the illuminative way.

The illuminative way involves us in a further growth in this life, which by analogy is compared to the physical growth of a human being. A human being begins in childhood, but when they begin to adopt the other perspective toward the world—when the sexual urge, for example, begins to grow in them, when their bodies grow in a certain sense, and their emotions begin to be more fully realized in their intelligence—they enter what's called adolescence and then the teenage years. Teenagers have no identity, in a sense. They are not children anymore, so they can't be treated like children, and they don't respond to the pleasures and pains that adults might often use to get children to do what they want them to do. On the other hand, they're not quite formed well enough yet to be adults, so you can't leave them with the idea that they're totally responsible for everything they do with no guidance, no direction, and no obedience.

They can't be treated like children anymore; you could say, in a certain sense, that they're crucified between childhood and adulthood. They have a foot in each, and yet they're in neither state. As a result, they have a loss of identity: they do not exactly know who they are spiritually.

The Experience of Spiritual Aridity

A similar thing happens in the spiritual life. When God begins to take us at our word, when He begins to give us a great influx of divine knowledge, which is faith; and divine love, which is charity; and of hope, we begin to be elevated in our perspective toward the world, just as the child is elevated out of childhood. The trouble is that we're not used to this; it's not our way of looking at things. We experience this as a great crucifixion, because what began for us as a loving, emotional, perhaps almost a honeymoon experience of God, enters a period of complete aridity. We become dry as a desert within. We might feel that God is far from us.

This points to an important spiritual truth: we cannot judge our progress in prayer by how we feel about it. There's nothing wrong with feelings; remember, God made the passions. Feelings are very poor indicators of maturity. A person may feel dry and arid, and yet be in great communion of life with the person whom they feel dry and arid about. And this is especially true of our relationship with an infinite being.

It is analogous also to living in a foreign country. I lived in Italy for six years and did business with Italian businessmen. I was in charge of the money in our community, the largest community in the order in Rome. When I went to that country, I could barely speak Italian. I sort of picked it up as I went along. Those people could have been saying to me, "You are the most wonderful person on earth. I love you. I want to have a deeper union of life with you," and all I would have heard would have been unintelligible. It could have been a depth of communication on their part, but I experienced it as a lack of communication on mine, because I hadn't become used to the way they communicate. It was only as I went along and became more accustomed to the way they communicated in their culture that I began to be able to translate certain words and phrases and to experience a deeper union with them.

What happens in the spiritual life is that God begins to communicate Himself to us in His language—in the language proper to the way the Father, the Son, and the Holy Spirit know and love each other in the Trinity—but we are bowled over by it. It makes no sense to us, because we have not learned yet what it means to know as God knows and to love as God loves. It's like wandering in a foreign country.

The Two Dark Nights

What we must do is learn receptivity—to learn to receive. We enter what the Carmelite mystics call "the two dark nights." The first dark night is a night of the senses. In this night, all our feelings about God that began so sweetly in our conversion experience are withdrawn from us, because God does not want us to love Him just because He makes us feel good. He wants us to love Him for what He is. In this dark night, our egoism finally begins to be consumed. It's like clipping off the weeds that grow around the action of the seed.

Then this night gives way to a deeper night, called by St. John of the Cross "the night of the spirit." This night was so terrible for him that although he wrote a book about the "night of the senses," he couldn't really express what happens in the "night of the spirit." In the "night of the spirit," even the very concepts and thoughts we have about God begin to become purified, and soon we realize that they fall short. These nights are a sign of our maturity. In fact. this deepening presence of God is experienced as an absence of God, because from our point of view we haven't learned yet how to understand what He's trying to tell us. Like the adolescent, we often feel that we've almost lost our soul, our identity, which is not the case. So, in this second great way of prayer, God is elevating us to His idea of things, but one does not perceive it as an eleva-tion. Instead, it seems like a desertion. Yet we are advised to keep living the life of prayer that we have always lived, because we're not actually deserted. In reality, God is beginning to purify us to experience Him in the way that He desires for us.

The illuminative way is the second great way of prayer, a kind of spiritual adolescence in which God begins to elevate us so we truly experience a communion of life with the Holy Trinity. Yet we experience this deeper presence of God as an absence. We might say to ourselves, "Was there ever a soul as dry as mine? I'm wandering in a spiritual desert. I can't understand or get around it inside." As Father Dubay stresses in his book *The Fire Within*, this is not the same as a psychological problem. It's not the same as one experiencing difficulties within because of emotional conflicts, because it's not a matter of a true absence. It is actually a deeper experience of God perceived as an absence. The person is happy and can focus his or her attention on everything—except he or she cannot seem to pray to God in the same way as before, perhaps because he or she was using a method.

Some people, perhaps influenced by Eastern meditation techniques, have suggested that in order to experience this dark night we must sit and willfully drive all concepts from our mind as if to produce a blank slate. In *The Interior Castle*, St. Teresa of Avila says that there are people who suggest that when we reach deep states of prayer, we should not think about Our Lord and Our Lady. This state they tell us to seek is called *quietus*, one in which we have no thoughts, no brains, no emotions, nothing. Saint Teresa writes, "As for people who speak this way, words fail me." Our Lord and Our Lady are the means by which we experience this level of contemplation. We do not turn this on and off by some technique. It's not some altered state of consciousness, although superficially the language that discusses it may bear such a resemblance. This is a deep interpersonal union and communion of spirits and hearts. It's not a matter of our wills as to when we experience God's presence or not. We merely open ourselves. As St. Teresa says, "The person should do and use their brains, as God gave them their brains to use to think about Him. If God wants to give us another way of thinking about him, that's his task to do, but not ours."

The prayer of quiet, or the prayer receptivity, are our doing; but the illuminative way and the dark nights are not things we produce. They are not a product. Instead, they are things that God works in us. All we can do is remain open.

Light and Darkness

It seems odd that this way is called in academic books the "illuminative way," and yet is characterized by two "dark nights"? Doesn't this seem contradictory? What do we do when we illuminate a room? We turn on lights. How can something be light and dark at the same time? When the sun is shining, go outside and try to look into the sun. We can't do that for very long. If we did, our eyes would become blind. Remember the days we would have our picture taken and the flashbulb would flash in our eyes? We'd blink and be temporarily blinded—not due to an absence of light, but because the presence of light was so intense that our eyes were too weak as receivers to take it all in or appreciate it.

A similar thing happens in this way of prayer. The presence of God, of His truth, of His love that is so infinite, is so intense that our weak human spirits can't take it all in. That's why people who used to talk about these ways of prayer in spiritual adolescence would quote, oddly enough, the pagan philosopher Aristotle in this regard. Aristotle used to say, "Before the deepest things of the world, the mind of man is like the eye of the bat or the owl looking into the sun." Bats and owls are creatures that inhabit dark places, either the night or caves. Their eyes are very weak. When they fly out into the bright sunlight, they are blinded—not for a lack of light, but because of a superabundance of the presence of light.

The same is true in this experience of prayer. We experience this as a desert: "was there ever a soul as dry as mine?" The Psalmist says, "Be strong and wait for the Lord" (Ps 27:14), but what are we waiting for? We are waiting for the person praying to get used to the new manner in which God elevates us to His way of knowing and loving.

How does one tell the difference between an interior darkness caused by sin, which is an absence, and an interior darkness caused by blindness to the bright life, which is a presence? If we are relatively sure we are in the state of grace because we are not conscious of having committed grave sin, have been to confession, practice our religion, and know God is present there, then what are we waiting for? We're waiting to become used to the way He communicates Himself in His way, and not the way we would have Him communicate Himself.

Obviously, this involves a deep surrender of the ego. To say that we must be willing to open ourselves in order to allow God to elevate us in His way means we must lose ourselves. It's a great suffering, but it's a suffering joyfully born from love because we are slowly being transformed into Him. It's like the weeds not only being clipped off, but pulled out at the roots, the weeds of our egotism and our pride.

Why does God allow this to happen to us?

Glory through Brokenness

There's a little Chinese legend about a bamboo tree, which is hollow inside if you root it out: Once upon a time there grew a beautiful and noble bamboo tree, which was the most beautiful and most beloved inhabitant of the master's garden. Year after year, Bamboo grew conscious of his master's love and delight but remained modest and gentle nonetheless. Often, when winds came to revel in the master's garden, Bamboo would play right along merrily, dancing and swaying and bowing in joyous abandon.

One day, the master of the garden drew near to contemplate his bamboo with eyes of curious expectancy. He said, "Bamboo, Bamboo, I would use you."

Bamboo flung his head to the sky in utter delight, for the day of days had come, the day in which he would find his completion and his destiny. He said, "Master, I'm ready. Use me as you will."

"Bamboo," the master said, "I would take you and cut you down."

A trembling of great horror shook Bamboo. "Cut me down? Me, the most beautiful in all your garden, and you would cut me down? Not that, not that! Use me for your joy, but do not cut me down."

"Bamboo," said the master, "If I don't cut you down, I can't use you."

Then Bamboo was bowed to the ground. He said, "Master then cut and cleave. Cut me down."

Then the master said, "Well, Bamboo, I have to strip from you your leaves and branches."

"Strip me from my leaves and branches?" Bamboo replied. "Would you lay my beauty in the dust and strip me?"

"Bamboo, if I don't strip you, I cannot use you."

So Bamboo said, "Then master, strip me."

Then the master said, "Ah, but Bamboo, to use you I have to take you and cut out your heart. For if I cut not so, I cannot use you." Then was Bamboo bowed to the ground. And he said in his humility, "Master, then cut and cleave."

So did the master of the garden take Bamboo and cut him down and cut off his leaves and strip off his branches and cut out his heart. And lifting him gently, he carried him to where there was a spring of fresh sparkling water in the midst of his dry fields. He put one end of the broken bamboo into the spring and the other end in the irrigation water channel in the field, and the water raced joyously down Bamboo's torn body into the waiting fields.

Then the rice was planted, and the days went by, and shoots grew, and the harvest came. In that day was Bamboo, once so glorious in his stately beauty, yet more glorious in his brokenness and humility, because in his beauty he was life abundant, but in his brokenness and humility he became a channel of abundant life to his master's world.

The world is thirsting for grace. When we allow Christ to break us down, when we allow Him to elevate us in His perspective, what He wants to do is replace our heart, our way of loving, with His sacred and wounded heart, His way of loving, so that we can truly become a channel by which we participate in the bringing of the grace of the crucified Lord to this world.

Spiritual Maturity

Following spiritual infancy and spiritual adolescence—the purgative way and the illuminative way—we come to the final experience of the communion of the soul with God, called the unitive way. Two points require emphasis here.

The first point is that although mystical authors often write of these things using very ethereal terms, this is not an ethereal experience. It is an experience of ordinary people in ordinary places in ordinary life with the ordinary virtues connected to the duties of their state but performed, as Christ would have us do, from the perspective of divine love.

The second point is this: grace is a seed given to us in baptism, and God never gives any seed, either in nature or in our moral lives, without the purpose of it producing a fully mature plant. A similar thing is true of the life of grace that each of us has received. Every single baptized person, not merely some select spiritual elite, is called to fullness of the experience of grace, to "set our hearts." As St. Paul writes, "If then you have been raised with Christ, seek the things that are above, where Christ is, seated at the right hand of God." (Col. 3:1). He doesn't say, "Monks, nuns, and priests, set your heart on higher things"; we also must do this in our way of life. When St. Paul says, "If then you have been raised with Christ," he refers to us all, as every single one of us has been raised with Christ through Baptism. He also says "*Conversatio nostra in Caelum est* " ("Our conversation is in Heaven"). Here he doesn't mean in the physical sense necessarily, but rather the interior conversation that each of us has in our conscience with God. That has to take place in Heaven, which means that we must adopt the heavenly perspective toward the world. That is why grace was given to us.

Betrothal To God

So when a person in spiritual infancy begins to practice the virtues and root out their faults, when God takes them at their word in spiritual adolescence and He begins to communicate His light and His love in His way, and this takes root in the person, the person enters into the final experience. The prophet Hosea writes:

> Therefore, behold, I will allure her, and bring her into the wilderness, and speak tenderly to her. And there I will give her her vineyards, and make the Valley of Achor a door of hope. And there she shall answer as in the days of her youth, as at the time when she came out of the land of Egypt. "And in that day," says the Lord, "you will call me, 'My husband,' and no longer will you call me, 'My Baal.' ... And I will betroth you to me for ever; I will betroth you to me in righteousness and in justice, in steadfast love, and in mercy. I will betroth you to me in faithfulness; and you shall know the Lord." (Hos. 2:14-16, 19-20)

These words are spoken by the prophet to Israel. But because Christ was a member of Israel, and we as members of His Church are members of the New Israel, these words have also been spoken to us in the desert of our hearts. Israel was allured into the desert after the Exodus, and God spoke to her heart in the Old Law. Now God speaks to our heart, to the New Israel in the New Law of Christ, which is not written on tablets of stone but on the heart itself by the gifts of the Holy Spirit. The spousal love God showed Israel is completed in the spousal love each soul enjoys from grace.

In fact, in the final great way of prayer, the unitive way, spiritual maturity, St. Teresa says we experience first of all a *mystical courtship*, then a *mystical betrothal*, and then a *mystical marriage*. In the mystical courtship, our wills are filled with God. In the mystical marriage, our intelligence is filled with God. And in the mystical marriage, even our very passions are full of God, so that we can look at the world from God's perspective.

An Eternal Perspective

The new perspective which God causes in us is expressed: "*Respice omnia sub aspectu aeternitatis*" ("Regard everything under the aspect of eternity"). This is what happens to us when we allow the fullness of grace to enter our souls. We begin to know as God knows, and love as God loves. We begin to regard everything from eternity. We begin to be changed, in a new way of knowing in which absolutely everything now is looked upon from God's perspective, which is really a perspective of faith.

If we were to read Thomas Aquinas' five proofs of the existence of God from the perspective of reason, we would start with material creation we experience by the five senses in everyday life and ascend from the effect to the cause Who is the Creator. But in the perspective of faith, we begin with the Creator. We begin with the Trinity. We begin with God, and we look down at the whole world, at the whole of time, as God does. This is the perspective of faith.

Mother Julian of Norwich, an English mystic in the Middle Ages, had a vision of Christ who held in his hand a little thing the size of a hazelnut, a very small nut. She said to him, "Lord, what is this that you are showing me?" And He said, "It's everything that exists. It's all of time and all of space as God regards it." She said she marveled that it could last because it was so small. And He said to her, "It lasts, as it ever does, because God loves it." This is the perspective that we are introduced into in the unitive way. Like a mystical marriage, we experience an exchange of hearts with the Lord. At the beginning, all God gave us to understand of His life caused confusion because we didn't understand it. But now we really appreciate what it means to stand back and look at the world from the divine perspective. This new way of knowing gives us a new appreciation of things.

One of the Psalms says, "In thy light do we see light" (Ps. 36:9). When we truly look at the world from the perspective of faith, each of us should see our spouse, our children, our job, our life, our good points, our strengths, our weaknesses, all those things as God so regards them. God regards them each as something that means to discover a deeper relationship with Him, if only we would allow Him to elevate us to this relationship.

A New Way of Living—and Loving

So now we also have a new way of loving in which our delight in the world and in others takes on a whole new perspective, where we love others as Christ loves them. This new way of loving offers to us a whole new perspective as to how to carry on our lives, how to live by our virtues, how to love without expecting return, just as Christ so loved. We sometimes say other people have to be perfect in order for us to love them: "I won't love you unless you're perfect." Well, Christ didn't expect us to be perfect when He loved us. He died on the Cross despite our imperfections. It's true that God's love is different than man. In man's love, we must find something lovable in order to love it. This calls forth from us our will. With God's love, however, God creates the lovability in the beloved. We are the result of divine love just by the fact that we exist. He loves us into existence, and He also loves us into salvation. The deprivation neurotic may intellectually know these things but emotionally finds them hard to accept. Since their whole experience is formed by love based on usefulness, they have a hard time accepting that they are loved disinterestedly by God.

Many practical fruits in action elude those who are not disinterested. There are deeper ways of looking at virtues that this way of love can call forth from us. For example, a very deep sign in ordinary life of this divine love is the ability to forgive another person. We expect God to be merciful to us, but we are very merciless toward other people.

The parable that is clearest about this, the one that should strike each one of us through the heart when we read it, is the parable of the heartless debtor (see Matt. 18:23-35). The heartless debtor went to the king owing a small fortune, but couldn't pay. The king was going to hand him over to the torturers and put him in prison. The man besought the king, saying, "Have patience with me, and I will pay you all." The king's heart was moved with pity, and he forgave the whole debt. From there, the heartless debtor went out, found a fellow servant who owed him a few bucks, but this servant couldn't pay. The fellow servant used the exact same words to plead his case: "Have patience with me, and I will pay you all." But the heartless debtor would hear none of it. "Bind him over to the torturers," he said, "till he pays back what he owes." When the king found out what had happened, he called the heartless debtor. And he said, "You worthless wretch. I forgave you an infinite debt, because you besought me, and you couldn't forgive your fellow servant even a tiny fraction of that?"

The one who wants to receive mercy must show mercy. Forgiveness of others which is true is one powerful action of mercy.

Difficulty With Forgiving

One of the problems many people have in forgiving, which is an adult and complicated act, is the result of one of two extremes regarding anger. Anger is the natural passionate response of self-restraining love to perceived injury. People either lose their tempers and act irrationally, or they simply deny that anyone offends them and thereby enable others. Both are equally inhuman because they are contrary to the reason anger exists: the emotional support for one trying to bring about the correction of the wrongdoer. The Stoical reaction would maintain that all anger is evil. Yet the Scriptures do not say that. Instead, they say things like "do not let the sun go down on your anger" (Eph. 4:26). Yet, as we have seen, they also teach against the other extreme, anger to the point of desiring revenge: "Be angry but do not sin" (Eph. 4:26).

Virtue stands in the middle. One should learn in childhood not to suppress the emotion of anger as an obsessive-compulsive but should also be taught to feel it in a human way. The affirmation neurotic would think that they deserved all evil done against them and simply not react with anger. The correction of the wrongdoer must be the primary purpose of the feeling of anger. In our present emotionally deprived society it is important to point out that when a person cannot feel anger, he or she is easily victimized by evil and does not resist.

There is difference, then, between the feeling of anger and its expression. One must be able to feel anger at evil. At the same time, one must not allow the feeling to distract from correction of the wrongdoer. This may, at times, demand mercy. The wrong-doer may be dead but may somehow be pushing the buttons of the offended party from the grave. We can allow such feelings of unresolved anger to destroy us, or we can make a conscious choice to forgive. Only the latter will set us free from being enslaved by the wrongdoer. Neurotic personalities need to be freed from this again in order to be proper moral agents. Therapy must have freedom from anger as its goal because it returns order and peace to the interior self.

The Power of Mercy and Forgiveness

Mercy and forgiveness of others are signs of the transformation of heart that grace causes in the character. Freedom to forgive includes freedom to feel angry and not to be held in bondage by the wrongdoer. Saint Thomas Aquinas asks in one of his books if it's possible for us to merit the first grace for another human being. He says, "No one can merit the first grace by strict equal-ity from God." Catholics do not believe that our works, by strict equality, can merit anything. But Thomas says that if we love God because we experienced this exchange of hearts with him, then God loves us. And he puts it in an interesting way: "By our propor-tion equality, we do our part as man does God's will. God wants to do man's will."

In this proportion equality, therefore, it's possible for us to be the means that God uses. Our forgiveness, for example, can be the means God has chosen to bring about the conversion of another. The classic example is from Scripture. Saint Stephen, as he was being stoned in the Acts of the Apostles, prays, "Lord, do not hold this sin against them" (Acts 7:60). And the book of Acts specifically remarks that the people stoning Stephen piled up their coats at the foot of a man named Saul, who concurred in the act of killing. Yet not shortly thereafter, Saul had a conversion experience and became St. Paul. Christian theology had always attributed the conversion of St. Paul to the prayer of Stephen, that God would forgive those who killed him.

"I Forgive You"

I suppose the most graphic example of this in the contemporary world involves St. Maria Goretti. She was a young girl who lived in Italy at the beginning of the twentieth century. She was very poor; her father died when she was a baby. Because of poverty, she and her family were forced to live with another family. They were peasants who worked in the fields. But remember that ordinary people, even unlettered people, are called to this fullness and depth of grace.

When she was about 12, as she was preparing for First Communion, a catechist explained to her what sin was. She was so boiled over by the horror of sin that she said, "I never want to commit a sin in my whole life." So, before she received her First Communion, she went to every member of the family and asked their forgiveness for anything she may have done against them.

There was a boy in the other family who lusted after her. His name was Alessandro, and he was just a little older than she was, maybe thirteen or fourteen. He kept trying to persuade her to have sexual relations with him, but she kept refusing him. He was so full of lust that he said to himself, "The next time she refuses me, I'll kill her." One day, Alessandro was working in the fields, and Maria was at home babysitting the children. Alessandro stole away from the group, went home, and accosted Maria. She refused him. Then, with an iron stake, he savagely stabbed her 14 times. What was she saying while she's being stabbed? Did she say, "Alessandro, I hope you go to hell forever for what you're doing me"? No, she said, "Alessandro, don't do this. It's a sin and I want you to be with me in Heaven." Maria lingered on for almost a day. The priest brought her the last sacraments and told her, "You know you're a Christian. You have to forgive him." She said, "Father, not only do I forgive him, but I pray he'll be with me in Heaven."

The crime was very notorious in Italy. Alessandro was sent to prison, and he was full of self-loathing. He refused all kinds of consolation of religion. Then one day he had a vision of Maria Goretti dressed in white with fourteen lilies. He took this as a sign that he had been forgiven, and he began to practice his faith. Years later, Alessandro was released from jail, but the crime was still very notorious. He was fired from every job he found, and he had almost despaired of life, when one day he received an invitation to work at the rectory in the parish where Maria Goretti was buried. He went to the rectory and knocked on the door. The housekeeper opened the door, and the housekeeper was Maria Goretti's mother. Alessandro knelt down and beseeched her in tears to forgive him. And Maria's mother said, "As we hope to be forgiven before God, if my daughter can forgive you, I forgive you."

That night they both received Communion in the shadow of Maria's tomb. Years later, he testified for her cause for canonization, but he was not present at her canonization Mass out of concern for his safety. Alessandro became a Franciscan, a Capuchin brother. A journalist interviewed him before he died and asked, "Do you despair of your salvation because of what you did to that girl?" And Alessandro replied, "But for her prayers and her forgiveness, I would despair of my salvation." *"Alessandro, don't do this. It's a sin and I want you to live with me forever."*

Surrender of Self

This experience of self-surrender is open to us, but we are not often open to it. Saint John of the Cross, reflecting on why more people don't have this experience, said, "O souls created for such wonders, what are you doing with your time? Your aims are base and your possessions miseries. O wretched blindness of your eyes, your blindness so brilliant to light and deaf to such loud voices because insofar as you seek eminence and glory you remain unworthy of so many blessings."

We must realize the depth and dignity to which grace can bring us if only we are open to it. It involves nothing less than the surrender of ourselves to God so that we may become a channel of faith and grace to the world as we participate in God's own conversion of the world. We must allow ourselves to experience this grace. We must open ourselves more and more to the healing of our spirits so that we might live out our ordinary relationships with extraordinary love. After all, isn't this the spirituality of the Little Flower, St. Therese of Lisieux?

In progressive healing of the spirit, true spiritual maturity is open to all of us if only we would allow Christ to do this for us. This is wonderful and deep. This is something so great that is offered to us, it would be a shame if we were to miss it.

When we allow this ordinary spirituality to enter our life, then He betroths us to Him forever in righteousness, justice, steadfast love, mercy, and faithfulness. In that way, we shall come to know the Lord.

There are lots of virtues—prudence, justice, temperance, fortitude, faith, hope, charity, and all kinds of others. We have an opportunity to practice these every day, all day, in every situation, so that we might truly experience spiritual healing and form ourselves in true spiritual integrity, to experience a wholeness of God within.

8

Prevention of Neurosis

Attitudes to Family and God

Since the deprivation neurosis is characterized by an underdevelopment in the passions caused by a lack of reasonable direction in childhood, and repressive neurosis is caused by and emotional conflict based on bad moral instruction, it is the task of the therapist to supply reasonable guidance for the passions. In other words, the therapist is seeking in an accelerated way the normal development of the passions through childhood and adolescence that the person did not experience because of inadequate education and an emotionally deprived childhood. A similar role is important for the repressive neurosis. Obviously, since issues of authentic authority are important here and religion and family often play a role in these issues, the whole question of how one emotionally relates to God and others must be examined. Human beings form their usefulness judgement or estimative sense emotionally through the intellect. The prevention of emotional illness is thus intellectually based.

First, as to human love, it is important to distinguish between volitional and emotional love. There are two levels of love in man. In a mature person, they must be combined. "In general the word 'love' signifies the feeling of attraction or, as St. Thomas Aquinas called it, the sense of affinity (*complacentia*) that one feels in relation to the good perceived in some person or thing." This means that in a completely integrated movement of human love, both will act together. Volitional love in itself is caused by a judgment of the intellect and does not include the passion of love. We can *will* the good to God or another even with a feeling of indifference or aversion on the level of the passions. Nevertheless, "emotional love belongs to the perfection of human nature, and so much so that without it a person is not fully human; an integral part of human nature is lacking." For the passions to participate in this involves a virtue in which volitional love, which is other-oriented, is gradually introduced into the passion of love. Spontaneity results from this combination of the levels of love.

This attitude of love will reveal itself in tenderness and affirmation. This is not a manner of doing, unless actions are required, but rather an attitude of approval of the being of the other. When this attitude of approval is present, one often must refrain from expressions of love when they are inappropriate to the person or against the law of God. The expressions or acts may actually be in accord with the law of God, but the person may not be able to receive them.

The Need of Self-Restraint

In someone who is filled with other-centered love, this demands self-restraining love. This is not repression, but restraint. "Therefore, when an emotion arises which reason, not fear, decides should not be allowed to be gratified for the sake of another greater good, restraint must be exercised in the expression of this emotion without interfering in the experiencing of the emotion itself." "The need for self-restraining love may be twofold. First, when objectively considered, a particular manifestation of love is not a reasonable good—if, for instance, it calls for actions which conflict with the objective moral order. Second, when subjectively considered, the one loved is psychically incapable of a proper response to a certain manifestation of love."

Authentic family life is the place where a person first learns this self-restraint. Birth control, abortion, and divorce are three of the primary threats to the learning of this self-restraint in the modern world. Each robs all the participants in the family of learning affirmation and also self-restraining love in the correct way. Dr. Baars reflects psychologically on "one of the most successful campaigns in modern history...: the campaign of birth control. Successful [that] campaign had been, because birth control appeals so much to the selfish element in every human being. It eliminates the responsibilities and duties of love, it decries the consequence of romance, and it educates young people in their own selfish interest and in the indulgence of their selfish pleasures."

Abortion involves the mother's complete denial of the human worth of her child. "The destruction of innocent human life is the most extreme form of non-affirmation. Its effect on the mother is no less grave, since she destroys the very being which is destined to affirm her in its own unique way." True affirmation of a woman with an unwanted pregnancy requires assisting her in all the things needed to bring her baby to term.

Finally, regarding divorce, Dr. Baars considers it to be the primary cause in the contemporary world of psychological conflict and unrest. The family is tied together by natural physical bonds that intimately relate to the perfection of the human soul because of the soul-body union. These natural bonds are so strong that no artificial bond or parenting can completely compensate for them. "Foremost among the factors that weaken the natural family bond stands the most radical dissolution of marriage: *divorce*." Dr. Baars believes that the emotional trauma caused by divorce is worse than almost anything that can occur within the family itself short of the death or physical injury of the spouse.

Forging the Bonds of Family

These three practices are not only morally evil but also psychologically destructive. It is not enough just to keep the family together physically. "It should also *form a unit emotionally*." Both the mother and the father participate strongly in the intellectual and emotional development of their children. The mother's influence is especially important in the home; the father's is especially important outside the home. The mother's guidance is especially needed in primary years; the father's in adolescence. Both must concentrate on paying attention to the children. This does not mean always doing things with them, but rather showing true interest in important times and not passing off discipline to others. Parents must be true leaders, both spiritually and emotionally.

Dr. Baars is especially eloquent in his treatment of fatherhood, a role he considers to be very misunderstood and devalued in the present society. "Absent or weak fathers, especially those who are afraid of their wives, make it hard for boys and girls to become independent or self-sufficient and socially at ease with their peers and persons in authority." He thinks the father is the emotional and intellectual support to the mother, which allows her the emotional freedom to give herself to her children unreservedly. He quotes Homer: "Homer showed his deep understanding of the nature of woman when, in his famous lines in the *Iliad*, he had Andromache bid farewell to her husband, Hector, with the following words, 'Hector, you are to me all in one father, venerable mother and brother, you are my husband in the prime of your life.'".

The place of religion in emotional development is also very important. The truths of religion in themselves are good and right. Unfortunately, they have all too often been presented in too precon-scious or authoritarian a way. God is the most reasonable thing and also the greatest good. Though one should avoid evil, well- meaning educators often presented a God to children where *only* sin or asceti-cism was emphasized. Sometimes this bordered on body hatred. This is, of course, a heresy. To hate the body is Manicheanism, and to hate the passions is an extreme of Stoicism. Catholics believe man is wounded as a result of Original Sin, not totally depraved. The avoidance of sin is important because sin interrupts God's purpose, which is always positive. "God's purpose continues to be the same: to give all men and women the opportunity to share in His own ultimate happiness if they so freely will it." This means that religion is not in the business of manufacturing self-control merely through the passion of fear, but by a choice, one hopefully supported by the passions, by the love of Christ.

The Moral Freefall of Free Love

If the hatred of the body is morally wrong and psychologically destructive, so too is the worship of the body and the attempt to bring about emotional integrity by abolishing moral norms. Yet that is what many Catholic moral theologians and educators did in the '70s and '80s. Dr. Baars calls the attempt to empty of their sinful character practices like birth control, premarital sex, and masturbation "erroneous goings on".

Some examples of these erroneous ideas were Lawrence Kohl-berg's "Six Stages of Human Development," Sidney Simon's "Values Clarification" philosophy and the book *Guidelines to Human Sexuality*, commissioned in the '70s by the Catholic Theological Society of America, which taught that there were no moral absolutes, no acts which were always wrong, especially in regard to sexual acts. This teaching was confirmed by the whole school of Consequentialism censured by Pope St. John Paul II in his 1993 encyclical *Veritatis Splendor* ("The Splendor of Truth"). At least two generations of students in Catholic schools were harmed by these false teachings in Europe and America. It is no wonder there are so many emotionally inadequate people. Bad moral teaching that is emptied of sin causes bad psychological formation because only the truth can set man free.

"The 'revolutionary sexual health' philosophy which denies the possibility of sin is but the logical outcome of minds that refuse to recognize man as a spiritual being and deny the validity of objective moral norms." This cannot free contemporary man "from the loneliness and joylessness that is intrinsic to open marriages, casual sex, sexual exploitation, in short, *sex without self-restraining love.*"

Fatherhood and the Destruction of Individuality

Thus far we have been discussing the progressive maturity that brings a person's soul to be able to experience in everyday relationships the way God looks at the world, the way God knows the world, and the way God loves the world. Now we will apply this theoretical treatment to certain practical, everyday situations in which many people find themselves.

Since the ideal paradigm for how the soul relates to God is the spousal union of marriage, we will first examine how ideas concerning how the way God looks at the world could be applied to us in everyday family life.

Probably there is no institution in our society that is in greater trouble than fatherhood. The reason is the way we look today in our society first on general relationships among people and secondly on how we define masculinity. Bishop Fulton J. Sheen used to say that there was a thing in culture called the "lyricism of culture," by which he meant that a good idea in one part of the culture often became applied to all aspects of the culture in such a way that certain aspects of the culture that couldn't be submitted to that good idea were robbed of their important contribution.

One example of this in our culture is the whole idea of democracy. Democracy is a very good system of government. Unfortunately, in our culture, democracy has become not just a system of government but a philosophy of life—and a philosophy of life in such a way as to suggest that if everyone has a vote and everyone is considered to be equal in their vote in politics, that this means that every relationship is absolutely the same as every other relationship; that no person should ever try to be different in the way they relate to people, other than in the way other people relate to people; and that no one should ever strive for excellence in the way that he or she relates to people.

C.S. Lewis expressed this mediocrity in *The Screwtape Letters*, a fanciful correspondence of a senior tempter in hell to a junior tempter on earth about how to tempt someone away from Christianity. He writes of a toast that Screwtape proposes in hell over a banquet of souls that the demons are devouring. He apologizes for the banquet, because there's no crackling good food in these souls today like there used to be, because everybody had submitted to mediocrity. This mediocrity isn't just a good, but it's also an evil.

"Democracy is the word by which you must lead them by the nose," Screwtape says. "The good work which our theological experts have already done in the corruption of human language makes it unnecessary to warn you that they should never be allowed to give this word a clear and definable meaning. But the real end of this change in language is the destruction of individuality."

The destruction of individuality—the idea that no one should ever seek excellence or be different, that everybody has to be exactly the same—has many ramifications in our culture. One ramification is seen in fatherhood. In a 1995 book called *Fatherless America*, David Blankenhorn writes, "Today's expert story of fatherhood largely assumes that fatherhood is superfluous." In other words, if everybody is supposed to be exactly equal, then there's no difference between fatherhood and motherhood, and one parent suffices just as well as two parents, and two parents of the same sex suffice as well as two parents of different sexes. Parenting, in this view, has absolutely nothing to do with the sex of the parent and how that sex would relate to the child.

Of course, we have this problem today too because of radical feminism—and a radical feminism which occurs not just in the state, but even in the Church. I was reading recently a statement by a woman who attended a women's church conference in 1983 in Washington, D.C., Rosemary Radford Ruether. She said:

> We are Women-Church, not an exile, but an exodus. We flee the thundering armies of Pharaoh. We are not waiting for a call to return to the land of slavery and serve as altar girls in the temples of patriarchy. Our Brother Jesus did not come to this earth to manufacture this idol. And he is not represented by this idol. We cry out, 'horror, blasphemy, deceit, foul deed.' We call on people to flee with us from this idol with flashing eyes and smoking nostrils who's about to consume the earth. Together let us break up this great idol and ground it into powder. Dismantle the great leviathan of violence and misery and transform it back into the means of peace and plenty so that all children of the earth could sit together at the banquet of life.

The woman who put this quote in a book she wrote about the Church adds at the end of this quote, "Golly." People who feel this way will not be converted by changing a few pronouns.

God as a Model of Fatherhood

People have a great reaction against the whole idea of what father-hood means. This is shown in our objections that some people have today to men alone being priests. It's also shown by the attempt to reduce fatherhood and families to being nothing, and the attempt to make God's image as Father or Mother equal. We will look at each one of these things in succession.

Regarding the idea of God as a Father, it is true God does not have a body. What we do in our language and in our representa-tions is use concepts or ideas that we experience here on earth to express certain truths about God—always, of course, changing certain ideas about them. One example is fatherhood and mother-hood. When we say that God is a mother, what are we saying? The word for mother in Latin is *māter*, a word that relates to the word "material," which means "matter." What we do when we make God feminine is what many pagan religions that worship goddesses do: identify God with the material world. In other words, we are saying that there is no transcendence of God whatsoever, but rather He's the same as the earth. God is not "other." The earth is regarded as a mother and a goddess in pagan religions, so this tells us that God as mother is something that is not a spirit, but matter. The attempt to make God totally other—to say that He is spirit—comes from the term we use when we state that God is a Father.

In the Old Testament, God is portrayed as a Father. Jeremiah writes, "I am a father to Israel, and Ephraim is my first-born" (31:9). And we read in the Psalms, "Thou art my Father, my God, and the Rock of my salvation" (89:26). Though Jesus, of course, refers to God as Father many times in Scripture, in the Old Testament this is prescinding from His personal relationship to the Father in the Trinity; it's merely trying to say that God as a Father is a Spirit Who is almighty, and so it's an image of power. But it's also an image of power that's connected to benevolence. In other words, it is not the power of a grasping, jealous, egotistical being who wants to use his power to thwart us, trash us, or subject us to himself, but instead it's a power that is shown in the giving of the self to the other. After all, God's goodness is diffusive of itself, and His creation is a result of His gift.

It's true that the Old Testament provides certain images that express the motherhood of God, the feminine character of God, in the prophets, for example. These, however, are always inserted into the masculine image. What they're saying is that God is wholly *other* than the world, but He is not *divorced* from the world. He is intimately present to everything that exists, but He is not present to that thing as a part of its being. God is intimately present to a tree, because if He didn't will the tree into existence—if He didn't cause it to exist, and think of the tree existing—it would cease to exist, but He's not a tree.

Therefore, to say that God is present in the world and intimate to the world, which the mother image tends to emphasize, depends on God being transcendent to the world. After all, if God were in a tree, He could not be equally in a bush, or in a rock, or in a sunset, and He couldn't equally be in me, if He were part of the matter of a tree. The one that God is *not* is material. So, to say that He is transcendent but causes the thing to exist is to say that He is equally present to everything. God is *omnipresent*.

The Father's Perfect Image

This transcendent, benevolent God also shows fatherhood within the Holy Trinity because He brings forth His perfect image in His Son, the Word. The Word is the perfect image of the Father. The completion of the image of fatherhood as transcendent is seen in the fact that the Word in eternity is exactly like Him, and yet totally different in person. This image of the Father and the Son, of course, is used by Christ in His human nature to show a unique relationship of Fatherhood. This unique relationship is the one He has as a member of the Trinity. The affirmation of sublime benevolence and supreme caring—exemplified in God the Father as both the Creator and the Father of Jesus Christ—must serve as a model in our excessively egalitarian democratic world, where all differences tend to be glossed over, to recover a model of true fatherhood with us.

We are told in Ephesians that the father is the head of the wife as Christ is the head of the Church (cf. Eph. 5:23). The husband is the head of the wife and the head of the family. How is Christ the head of the Church? Recall the motto, "To serve is to reign. To reign is to serve." Christ is the head of the Church because we see obedience and love in Him perfected in surrender, in the gift of Himself for the good of another. Human fatherhood, therefore, shares first of all in the role of God as Creator by benevolence and power, but it is a power that is shown in service.

The father takes the place of God in the relationship. How is this seen? Because, with the mother, he participates in creating life. Saint Thomas Aquinas taught, using a text from Aristotle, that because it has a potential to become a spiritual, material being, a man, and because that potential is only completed in communion with God, the seed of a man has something divine about it. Thomas, oddly enough, quotes Aristotle's *Politics*, when he says, "Therefore there is something divine in human seed." The reason the seed exists, the reason it comes forth from the man, is to produce a creature who can experience communion with God, a communion brought forth to us in the baptismal font. The marriage union, then, in which the father intimately participates is therefore a creative union.

God's Creative Power and Fidelity

The order of authority that the father initiates cannot be perfected without the truth and the love that accompanies God's creation and a commitment in intimacy to his wife and to his children. In procreation, the father and the mother supply the matter, but God Himself creates the form. As a result, every creative relationship, because it has something divine about it, also has something sacramental or worshipful about it. In the old marriage ritual, the husband used to say to the woman, "With my body I thee worship, with all my worldly goods I thee endow." What he was expressing there was not that he worships his wife as he does God, but that their relationship is like a sacrament; there is something holy about it.

The father must also perfect this image as creator, as God does, by showing benevolent love to the other. How does a person show benevolent love to another? He shows benevolent love to the other by looking on the other as a second self and by realizing that "Greater love has no man than this, that a man lay down his life for his friends" (John 15:13). The father must show his love for is family by dying for them, by sacrificing himself for them, and not by taking them to himself or using them to assert his ego. Instead, he shows his love by giving of his ego in truth, love, and commitment to them. This is especially the case in teaching the truth and intellectual affirmation in adolescence. His spiritual presence is essential to the peace of the mother and the virtuous formation of the children.

Although it is true to say that wives should obey their husbands as Christ, they do not obey their husbands as slaves to a tyrant. The relationship is that of a wise governor to a free citizen. Remember, this passage begins by saying, "Be subject to one another out of reverence for Christ" (Eph. 5:21). It is love, it is grace, which is the key.

If the husband, for example, is a moral derelict, he has no inner strength on which his wife can rely. His manliness is increased in direct proportion to the extent that he could offer himself to help her as a person to come out of herself, to give herself in affection to others—in other words, to support her. If he looks on her only to stroke his own ego—which is an attitude of machismo—or if he becomes a tyrant, it is no wonder that she rebels. She can't find herself. She's not free to give herself to another. The two have not become one flesh.

Father as Priest in the Family

The family is a domestic church. Since both parents are baptized, they participate in Christ as priest, prophet, and king. This is the cornerstone of the priesthood of the laity. The priesthood of the laity as priest, prophet, and king is primarily realized in the Sacrament of Marriage. As a result, the father must take the lead in religion; he cannot leave this to his wife. Since he is the head, and in a certain sense, the wife is the heart, he must be the one who directs the religious experience of the family.

Saint Augustine used to begin his talks to fathers in families by addressing them as "my fellow bishops." The father could fulfill this role by leading the prayers with his children, taking them to Mass, perhaps sitting and explaining the Mass while they were watching it or participating in it. He is the primary religious educator who should discuss the basic principles in the *Catechism* with his children.

Not only should the father teach the truth, but he should also encourage virtuous formation in his children. In this effort, parents exercise their priestly roles by preparing their children to get to Heaven. This is their role in education. Men must participate in this initiative because the father establishes the norm for humanity. In our culture, because of our excessive democratization, masculinity has been reduced to fast guns, fast cars, fast fists, fast men, and fast women. Men who possess that kind of masculinity do not respect other persons, but instead they use other persons to stroke their own egos and to show their power and strength. True power and strength is demonstrated by giving of oneself to another in order to bring out the good that is present in the other. The man, however, must be brought into the home, because it is essential for all family members to feel his presence spiritually.

To be the head of a family is the greatest adventure in the modern world. No action hero in any film ever faced the challenges that a person confronts today in trying to support a good home—spiritually as well as materially—and to educate children. It should be the greatest adventure on earth. Unfortunately, it is the adventure in which many people absolutely refuse to participate because they find it too hard to give up their own ideas or their own pleasure.

Fatherhood and the Evangelical Counsels

Every father must practice poverty, chastity, and obedience according to the duties of his state, the *evangelical counsels*. A father practices poverty by serving his family. He practices chastity by not neglecting his wife in any sense. And he practices obedience by realizing that he's just one good in the midst of the broad good of the scheme of others. The father, you can say, as he takes the place of Christ, is looked upon by the woman to provide with her all that she's found in her own home.

In another excellent expression of spiritual fatherhood, General Douglas MacArthur once said: "By profession I am a soldier, and I take pride in the fact. But I am prouder, infinitely prouder, to be a father. A soldier destroys in order to build. The father only

builds, never destroys. The one has the potentiality of death, the other embodies creation in life. And while the hordes of death are mighty, the battalions of life are mightier still. It is my hope that when I am gone my son will remember me not from battle, but in the home, repeating our simple daily prayer, 'Our Father, Who art in Heaven.'"

Grace should increase the spiritual intensity and urgency of this most spiritual of states of life. In a person who has experienced a formation from normal psychology, the potential for happiness is immense.

9

Difficulties in Modern Society
for Spiritual Healing

Turmoil in the Home

Now that we've examined how ordinary spirituality supports parents in providing their children with good emotional formation and teaching virtuous behavior, we will look at how this is applied in family life. The ancient epic, *The Odyssey*, has much to do with authentic ideas about the family.

Homer, the Greek poet, showed a marvelous insight into human nature in his famous epic. *The Odyssey* is about Ulysses, the Greek hero who has left his family to fight in the Trojan Wars for ten years. His return from Troy takes him many years. While he is gone, his home has gone to rack and ruin. In Greek ideas, the public room of the house, what we would call the living room, was a room in which people could be admitted from the outside. The man basically held some authority in this room, but once a person entered the private rooms of the house, the woman held authority there.

In *The Odyssey*, the public room of the house is occupied by suitors for the hand of Ulysses' wife, Penelope, and they are creating chaos in the home. They're having drunken orgies constantly. There's hardly a quiet time in the home. In other words, the home is greatly disturbed. Penelope does not know if her husband is alive or dead, but she assumes that since he's been gone so long, and she hasn't heard anything, he must be dead. Penelope, who's a very wily person, promises that she will marry one of these suitors after she finishes weaving a tapestry. So, in the daytime she weaves the tapestry, but at night she takes out everything she's woven, so that it would take forever to finish the tapestry.

In the meantime, her son, Telemachus, is lost. He has no identity. He has a complete chaos spiritually within. He is this way because his mother is in turmoil; his mother is in turmoil because there's no peace in the home; and there's no peace in the home because there's no man to establish the rock of unity. Telemachus's father is not spiritually present to him; because his father isn't spiritually present, his mother isn't spiritually present either, and so as a child he experiences a complete inability to get it together.

This is similar to what Original Sin causes in our homes through our weakness that we still inherit because of that first sin. Remember that in grace we receive the character of conformity to Christ; we get back sanctifying grace. But we do not get back the marvelous gifts of integrity of Adam and Eve. Instead, we experience, first of all, a kind of warfare within. This interior warfare is often reflected in the warfare outside, the disturbance of the home. It is only when the father and the mother can become spiritually present again to the children—when they truly exercise their role in the home as loving, benevolent, and truthful guides—that the children can finally come to experience their identity again.

Discipline as Improvement

Our modern Western culture is very much against this. In education, for example, people are taught that the child is a philosopher in his own right. He should never be disciplined, some say, except to keep him from interfering with someone else's freedom. Years ago, when I took teacher training in Los Angeles alongside other grammar school or high school teachers, we had a roundtable where we would discuss various issues that occurred in the classroom. One of the subjects that came up was discipline. One teacher, a Lutheran who had been a Los Angeles city schoolteacher for 20 years, said, in echo of modern European philosophy and especially the philosopher Rousseau, "The child is an educational philosopher in his own right. Never teach him anything, just lead him to self-discovery. I think you discipline children to keep them from interfering with each other's freedom."

When it was my turn, and the teacher who was moderating the roundtable asked me, "Why do you think you discipline children?" I replied, "I think you discipline children to make them better." The woman who had made the original statement looked at me and she said, "Where did you ever get a ridiculous idea like that?" And I said, "You will find it in Plato and Aristotle." Well, the moderator started to laugh uproariously, and he said, "I've been waiting for twenty years for someone in this class to mention Plato and Aristotle. Thank you."

In other words, there's an objective nature to man. It is not all just about self-discovery. The whole purpose of education is to help a person find certain truths that they might not discover on their own, but once discovered, they will make their own. This is not only true in secular education, but it is true in the Christian family.

The Christian Family

Earlier in this book, it was stated that there is something divine about human seed because the human seed has a potential to become a spiritual material being, and that because man is a spirit, man's final purpose is communion with God in grace and vision of God in Heaven. There is something divine about him, and so the whole relationship that revolves around the bringing forth of new human life—the relationship of marriage—demands that this act be completed by the proper education of these children. Pope St. John Paul II wrote this in one of his apostolic exhortations, and it is reflected in the *Catechism of the Catholic Church* as well: "The right and duty of parents to give education is essential since it is connected with the transmission of human life. It is original and primary with regard to the educational role of others on account of the uniqueness of the loving relationship between parents and children. It is irreplaceable and inalienable, and therefore inca‐pable of being entirely delegated to others or usurped by others" (*Familiaris Consortio*, 36).

Spiritual Parenting: Emotional Affirmation

Spiritual parenting demands that parents be present to their chil‐dren as God is to all of us. Parents can do this in two ways. The first means of spiritual parenting is to emotionally affirm the goodness of the child. This is done especially in the primary years, and it's the special providence of the woman. It's not that the man isn't involved in this, but the woman should be more involved in this form of parenting, as when she shows affection in a disinterested way, in a self‐restraining love way—in other words, she affirms the good of the other, that "it's good that you exist, not because you make me feel good." She affirms the good of the other, by speak‐ing more through the language of affection than words, "You are good that you exist because you come from the hands of a loving Creator." The child emotionally receives the goodness of his own being. This is one essential and important stage in education. A mother who is uninvolved, cold, aloof, or clinging does not allow the child to emotionally receive the gift of himself.

The parents are the first evangelizers of their children and responsible for their education. We have this terrible problem today where parents drop their kids off at religious education classes at the parish or at the Catholic school, and they figure that absolves them completely of any role they have in the education of their children. They leave the education of their children, especially religious education, completely to others. But that's not right: parents are the primary catechists for their children. Pope St. John Paul II said they're the "first apostles." Parents practice the priesthood of the laity in evangelizing their children. They're the ones that should be the primary religious educators. Where should a child first learn his religion? On his mother's knee, and with his father's active interest. Christian parents, in order to exercise this role completely, need to understand their faith themselves. Yet we're dealing with generations of uncatechized adults who are raising uncatechized children. As a priest, it's almost impossible for me fully to take the place of an absent parent when it comes to religious education.

A constant theme of this book has been that emotional affirmation—which is not just being nice, but rather being truthful and fair—has to correspond with intellectual affirmation. This intellectual affirmation is primarily what parenting is about. The primary education that the mother and father are interested in is the spirit—education in the virtues.

The Virtue of Obedience

Once, in the 1970s, I gave an eleventh-grade class in a Catholic school a diagnostic test about their faith. These children all had attended Catholic school for eleven years. They didn't know how many sacraments there were; they could only write a few from memory. Only half the class could write the Hail Mary from memory.

Most did know the Lord's Prayer because they said it every Sunday. But it was sad how little these people knew about their religion.

I often tell parents that if their children fall away from the Church in adulthood, the most effective manner they can use to draw them back is by their own example. When we show a good example and we're happy about our lives, people are going to want to know why. If we're there for them when they really need to discuss matters that pertain to belief or values, then we can try to evangelize them further. Once children reach adulthood, however, they have a certain freedom about them, and oftentimes the more we try to impose our ideas on them, the more they resist. Example, however, is a difficult thing to resist. Saint Augustine once told St. Ambrose, "You converted me much more by your love than by your arguments." That is a powerful truth.

Parents are supposed to educate their children primarily in the virtues because it is the virtues by which we live the life of grace and prepare ourselves for Heaven. It is the virtues by which we begin to participate in divine worship here on earth, but a worship that is only completed and finalized in the eternal worship in which we hope to participate after death in Heaven. There is one virtue that's really important, and it is very little lived today, and that's the virtue of obedience.

Obedience is much more than just doing what one is told. Obedience means that a person internalizes a truth or a value spoken to them by another person. In other words, although obedience involves submitting one will to another, it involves this submission because a common truth is shared.

The word "obedience" comes from the Latin word *obaudire*, which means "to hear." There is a saying that "to hear is to obey." But hearing in this sense means much more than just physical hearing. It means internalizing the value that is offered. Today there is very little true obedience in the world. Obedience is a virtue that is greatly underestimated.

Anyone who is asked to obey someone else must be open and receptive to the person in authority. They do this because they must not only be able to see and hear the other person and understand the command, but they also must be emotionally receptive to the idea that the person in authority has their good in mind. Even if what's asked of them or commanded of them is a particularly difficult good, they must be able to see on some level how it fits into a greater good. In other words, if we are going to give up a private good of ours, we must be able to see how in some sense this fits into realizing the greater good of others.

Obedience and Children

Spiritual maturity must be born from a proper psychology of obedience. Dr. Baars has a masterful article in which he examines "The Psychological Aspects of Obedience." What follows is based on his analysis. One must keep in mind that this analysis is not a moral analysis, although this is presumed. It is rather a psychological analysis.

The whole concept of obedience is in jeopardy today. Since the ideals of the French Revolution took over in Europe and an exaggerated idea of independence in America developed, people have held obedience in disrepute. The secularization process in the West has increased this malaise. If there is a difficulty in the idea of obedience in the Church today it is because there is first a difficulty with the idea of obedience in secular culture.

It is important to remark that God never directly governs things in the world. He always does so through secondary causes. In the natural world, when two forces meet, the more powerful as to energy influences the lower as to energy, and the more powerful as to form imparts being to the less powerful as to form. In the moral universe, it is the more influential as to truth and good which guides the rest. Any human superior shares in God's governing not because the persons exercising the office in themselves are better, but rather they have power to direct the actions of another because they represent the common good and speak according to the truth.

Since this direction is done by the intellect through the power of the will, St. Thomas Aquinas says: "Obedience is a special virtue, and its specific object is a tacit or expressed command." Any act of obedience, therefore, must be a complicated and adult act. It involves a number of intermingled attitudes.

On the part of the subject: (1) *Openness and receptivity.* The subject must emotionally be able to receive the command of the superior and to understand that the person in authority represents a good for the subject. (2) *Feelings of security.* Many people have been ill-served by authority, especially by domineering or neurotic parents when they were young. They find it hard to forsake a present good for a possible future good not yet possessed. They cannot surrender easily. This surrender is necessary if there is to be true obedience. (3) *Recognition of one's limitations.* It is natural for everyone, in whatever society, to be subject to another, because no human being can possess everything necessary for their own perfection in themselves. They depend on others for many things. A person who understands this does not obey merely out of fear of the consequences. This might be fine for children, but not for adults. Such a person obeys because he or she realizes that is just part of a greater and all-encompassing common good. (4) *Realization of one's dependence.* True obedience results from the understanding that the world does not revolve around the ego of the person obeying. The person's good includes the good of many others. Though the person appreciates their self-worth, they also understand their relative place regarding God, the world, and other people. (5) *Respect for authority*. This respect is not based on any particular individual quality of the person in authority, but rather on the common good they represent. One is ennobled and so becomes better in pursuing a higher good.

Those in authority need to understand that the very fact of obedience is a great sacrifice on the part of the one obeying. As a result, Saint Thomas quotes Pope Saint Gregory the Great: "He who forbids his subject any single good, must needs allow them many others, lest the souls of those who obey perish utterly from starvation through being deprived of every good." Thomas comments: "Thus the loss of one good may be compensated by obedience and other goods." Adults should understand that they are compensated by the loss of one good with the attainment of much higher, deeper, and metaphysical goods. In religious life, this would, of course, be the good of Christ, the community, and the Church.

There are children in whom this openness is seriously impaired in early life, and these children become completely egocentric. Their social development is disturbed, because they have been asked or been commanded to do things by people whom they perceive don't love them and don't care about them. They manifest this perception in their own halting way by practicing disobedience.

In other words, for a person to give commands and to try to encourage children to obey, the child has to be given the idea, at least in other areas of life, that this person is asking them to obey because they are interested in their good. If children are asked to obey merely to satisfy the ego of the person giving the command, this is impossible.

True versus False Obedience

As we've noted, the word "obedience" comes from the Latin *obaudire*, which means "as a result of hearing." The hearing spoken of here is an interior hearing, a consideration in conscience. The intellect must always be involved in directing the will; obedience cannot simply be a matter of willpower being controlled by emotion.

For this reason, Dr. Baars distinguishes many kinds of false obedience. These would include acts that mask as true obedience, because their resemblance to acts of true obedience is only superficial. Though a person may avoid sin in doing such acts of obedience, he or she does not implement or grow in the virtues or vows in doing so.

These include: (1) *Exaggerated servility.* This is a kind of submission to authority serving only to quiet an emotional fear of the consequences of disobedience. The superior might react negatively. There is no personal responsibility of choice of the good involved here. (2) *Identification with the person of the superior.* Though emotional identification with a person of authority is natural for children, it is not natural for adults. Adults can appreciate the various possible goods involved in obedience despite the person who commands. This is what "blind obedience" means. It does not mean stupid obedience. Rather, the good can be embraced regardless of any personal rapport with the one who commands it. Sometimes this form of obedience results from deprivation neurosis. One wants the mother and father one never had. (3) *Submission from repression.* One obeys here because it is efficient. A cold and unfeeling superior can stimulate excessively utilitarian activity in the subject. Of course, one who obeys for this reason is satisfying an overstimulation of the emotion of courage and finds it hard to obey when another superior is not so efficient. Religious life is often not that efficient, so this leads to frustration. (4) *Abdication of responsibility.* Here one obeys to put the responsibility for the act on another. This is not only immature, but also very adolescent. An adult takes responsibility for what he or she does. This form of obedience is practiced by one who wants to be a perpetual child. (5) *Obeying to shame others.* Here one has the model religious, but like the Pharisee with the Publican, one does not obey from love of the good, but just to show one's superiority. Sometimes the person even has a positive contempt for others.

Obviously none of these kinds of obedience fits the bill. The reason is that they are not acts of free human choice but rather result from an immature desire to satisfy some emotional need. One must remember that the purpose of obedience is to surrender the direction of one's life to another because of the temptation to dominate others. One seeks to avoid pride. It is almost impossible to be truly obedient and proud at the same time. Though one surrenders one's freedom of choice as to alternatives, one does not surrender the choice of an adult. One does not cut out the will and replace it with the will of another.

Finally, Dr. Baars examines the correct requirements of superiors. He first makes it clear that fraternal authority—authority by committee, in effect—is impossible. This represents an abdication of authority. The superior instead must implement the common good personally, and the subject must accept his authority personally. There is not true obedience to a committee.

The requirements for the superior are: (1) *Benevolent love.* The superior must generally have an attitude in which he or she communicates that the good of the subject is important to them. This must be more than an act of the will. Of course, this is again more an attitude of being which includes the emotions. The superior can demonstrate this by showing tact and patience and an understanding that there is risk to the subject in obedience. (2) *Respect for the subject.* The subject is not just an object of use but like every human person must be a subject of love, even when correction is needed. Of course, commands against the moral order should never be considered here. (3) *Avoidance of foolish and excessive commands.* No one can obey too many laws. The more detailed the instructions, the more difficult it becomes for the subject to rise to the occasion. Much latitude must be left to the prudence of the formed religious. After all, this is the purpose of a formation program. When any superior makes a subject slavishly dependent on them for every choice, this is either because the subject is badly formed, or the superior is abusing his authority. (4) *Prudence.* One cannot treat everyone in the same way in a community. Superiors should be alive to the personality differences in their subjects. Prudence demands that each person needs to be approached according to his or her particular personality.

Spiritual maturity in the love of Christ is the purpose of obedience. A mature superior who realizes this truth will always help a mature subject who also realizes this same truth to grow toward that final integration that only grace can bring.

Another condition for true obedience is that a person must recognize his or her own limitations. Every one of us must obey somebody in society. We must obey traffic laws, for instance, just to drive. We have our limitations as people. A person who doesn't have any limitations is not going to submit himself or herself to anyone else for guidance. If we have limitations, then we must depend upon others in order to be realized ourselves. There are people today who do not want to depend upon anybody. How can that be? We depend on all kinds of people for all kinds of things every day because we live in society.

This recognition of dependence demands that we have respect for those who command. This respect is not necessarily based on anything about their personality. It's based on the fact that they represent the common good to us, and we can perceive that they recommend the common good to us because what we really are obeying is the truth. Intelligence, then, is the most essential part of obedience.

Epilogue

The culture wars of the late 20th and early 21st centuries are characterized by a constant perception of interior emptiness and lack of higher
goods in the soul. The preoccupation is all with the satisfaction of
the autonomous self. Self-affirmation is caused by the reduction of
the desires of the interior soul to a materialism which promises human perfection but can only bring frustration. This frustration can
be expressed in emotional illness or even more in a spiritual illness
which is expressed in the unbridled and selfish need to affirm the
self at the expense of others. The *Los Angeles Times* expressed this
sad phenomenon in a cartoon about twenty-five years ago where one
man to another: "I compete, therefore I am; I manipulate, therefore
I am; I don't listen, therefore I am; I am therefore, you're not." The
self in today's world is self-created and thus denies not only truths of
reason such as the higher law of the Ten Commandments, but also
faith which is treated as subjective emotional satisfaction.

After surviving Buchenwald, Dr. Baars reflected on the problem
of the modern world and human healing and should be allowed
the last word:

Often I have been asked to explain how human beings
could degenerate so much that they were able to commit

such fiendish crimes. Conceited as I was in trying to appear as an intelligent man, I tried to answer this question with big words—sadism, inferiority/superiority complexes, mass suggestion, and so on. None of these words touches the core of the problem. There is only one answer, very simple in itself, but not always liked or appreciated by those who ask. *Evil flourishes because people no longer obey the laws and commands of God.* They no longer prayed and had put man and his finite intellect above God. It is a simple answer, but contemplate it and you will recognize its irrevocable truth. No one who lives in the grace of God COULD EVER commit such atrocities as this last war has seen.

Indeed it is a terrible truth and one which, at the same time, holds a solution to the future. We cannot live in peace, we cannot stay away from another war unless we return humbly to God and live as he wants us to live. There may be huge economic, political, and social problems that confront the world today which, if not solved will greatly endanger the peace, or rather the present state of not having an actual war. But all these problems are miniscule compared to the enormous problems of how to bring men and women back to God.[9]

---

[9]   Conrad Baars, *Doctor,* 186.

About the Author

Fr. Brian Thomas Becket Mullady is the son of an Air Force officer and was raised throughout the United States. He entered the Dominican Order in 1966 and was ordained in Oakland, California, in 1972. He has been a parish priest, high school teacher, retreat master, mission preacher, and university professor. He received his doctorate in sacred theology (STD) from the Angelicum University in Rome and was a professor there for six years. He has taught at several colleges and seminaries in the United States. He is currently a mission preacher and retreat master for the Western Dominican Province. He also teaches two months of the year at Holy Apostles Seminary in Cromwell, Connecticut. Fr. Mullady has had fourteen series on the EWTN Global Catholic Network. He is the author of four books and numerous articles and writes the answer column in *Homiletic and Pastoral Review*. He is also designated as an official Missionary of Mercy by Pope Francis.